Praise for Dream Exploration

"Who knows what a dream means? We dreamers do, as my colleague Robert Gongloff ingeniously demonstrates in *Dream Exploration,* a book bound to attract neophytes and experienced dream workers with the most practical and productive exercises I have ever read. Many dreamers find it difficult to mine the meaning of their dreams from the dark caves of the unconscious, but Robert leads us directly to the gold with his innovative focus on approaching the core of the dream, its very heart, its theme. While there are a proliferation of books on various approaches dreamers might follow to find the meanings of their dreams, Robert's concepts are a bold breakthrough from sifting through tortuous and sometimes misleading paths to the beneficial message the dream is delivering. He paves his route with concrete outlines, exercises, and examples, proving that the path of themes is the most direct route to the essence of the dream.

"Robert distills his own decades of dream work and his extensive studies in esoteric and ancient wisdom into easy-to-follow yet invaluable guidelines for working with dreams, helping us to discover what themes *are* but also what they *are not,* erasing popular misconceptions and replacing them with core themes that fit any dream or waking-life situation. With his genius for problem solving and clear organization of information, Robert has created a Theme Matrix, replete with twelve core themes that are common to all of us despite the varied aspects of our lives. We find ourselves challenged with pertinent questions that bring hidden issues to the light of consciousness."

—Rita Dwyer, past president and executive officer of the International Association for the Study of Dreams

DREAM EXPLORATION

www.artistwithcamera.com

About the Author

Robert P. Gongloff has been an active member of the International Association for the Study of Dreams (IASD) for fifteen years, including six years on the board of directors. He is a graduate of the Dream Leader Training program offered by the Haden Institute, and he has a master of arts degree in guidance and counseling from Wayne State University.

DREAM EXPLORATION

A NEW APPROACH

ROBERT P. GONGLOFF

Llewellyn Publications
Woodbury, Minnesota

First Edition
First Printing, 2006

Book design and layout by Joanna Willis
Cover design by Ellen L. Dahl
Cover image © 2005 by DigitalStock
Editing by Jane Hilken and Wade Ostrowski

Excerpts reprinted with permission from *The Creative Dreamer* by Veronica Tonay. Copyright 1995 by Veronica Tonay, Celestial Arts, a division of Ten Speed Press, Berkeley, CA. www.tenspeed.com.

Permission for use of material from *Tracks in the Wilderness of Dreaming* by Robert Bosnak granted by Nine Muses & Apollo Inc., New York, NY. © Robert Bosnak.

The publisher and author gratefully acknowledge Rita Dwyer for permission to use her name, words, and personal information about her life.

Llewellyn is a registered trademark of Llewellyn Worldwide, Ltd.

Library of Congress Cataloging-in-Publication Data
Gongloff, Robert P., 1940-
    Dream exploration: a new approach / Robert P. Gongloff.-- 1st ed.
        p. cm.
    Includes bibliographical references and index.
    ISBN-13: 978-0-7387-0818-8
    ISBN-10: 0-7387-0818-6
      1. Dream interpretation. I. Title.

BF1091.G657 2006
154.6'3--dc22   2005055250

Llewellyn Worldwide does not participate in, endorse, or have any authority or responsibility concerning private business transactions between our authors and the public.

All mail addressed to the author is forwarded, but the publisher cannot, unless specifically instructed by the author, give out an address or phone number.

Any Internet references contained in this work are current at publication time, but the publisher cannot guarantee that a specific location will continue to be maintained. Please refer to the publisher's website for links to authors' websites and other sources.

Llewellyn Publications
A Division of Llewellyn Worldwide, Ltd.
2143 Wooddale Drive, Dept. 0-7387-0818-6
Woodbury, MN 55125-2989, U.S.A.
www.llewellyn.com

Printed in the United States of America

We cannot discover new
oceans unless we have the
courage to lose sight of the shore.

—ANONYMOUS

This book is dedicated to all those
who have the courage to "lose sight of the shore"
by bravely exploring the mysteries of their dreams.

Contents

Acknowledgments

First and foremost, I want to acknowledge that my major exposure to the broad scope of dreams and the dream world has come through my affiliation with the International Association for the Study of Dreams (IASD). I believe I have learned more about dreams by rubbing elbows with IASD presenters and conference attendees than I could have in any number of dream books or coursework.

There are so many in the ever-growing dream community to whom I owe special thanks; the list would go on for pages. Many have not only been my teachers, supporters, and spirit guides, but I also consider them "family." I owe special thanks to Rita Dwyer, Robert Van de Castle, Jeremy Taylor, Carol Warner, Helen Carter, Chuck and Shirl Coburn, Bob Haden, Cody Sisson, Patricia Garfield, Rosemary Ellen Guiley, Erik Craig, Joanne Rochon, and Roberta Ossana.

Thanks to all of my spiritual teachers—especially Carol Parrish, Sonia Bergman, Carol Beyer, Betty Carper, and Alice Bailey.

Thanks to my favorite astrologer, Steve Nelson, who opened my eyes to the power of twelve.

Thanks to all the brave members of dream groups in which I have participated or that I led. I owe special thanks to Hugh and Joan Duncan and Deborah Coupey.

Thanks to my wonderful editors, Luann Fulbright (Fulbright Communications, McLean, Virginia) and Susan Snowden (Snowden Editorial Services, Hendersonville, North Carolina). Luann took what I see now was a random collection of ideas and gave me new direction and focus. Susan brought my words to life and guided me to the most effective presentation. They both had the overwhelming job of helping me understand what I was trying to say.

Thanks to Veronica Tonay and Robert Bosnak for allowing me to include their excellent techniques.

Thanks to the wonderful people at Llewellyn for giving me the opportunity to present my dreams to a broader audience.

And special thanks to my wife, Maria—my partner, my friend, my love—who encouraged and supported me through this adventure. She kept me inspired and on track. I could not have survived on chocolate alone.

The Need for a New Approach

Facts bring us to knowledge,
but stories lead to wisdom.

—RACHEL NAOMI
REMEN, MD

I go into a large library or bookstore that seems to offer options for what course I can take. A man is there who I believe is my teacher. He shows me a large book. It is very thick—approximately three inches wide—and is wrapped in cellophane or plastic. He says this is the one for me; I can order it. But I wonder about this book. Perhaps if it were a reference book with pictures or something, it would be easier to deal with. But I know it is all narrative, perhaps a long novel. Do I really want to take on something so large and complex without really being able to see what is inside the wrapping?

This was a dream I had in the summer of 2001. At the time, I was working with contractors and architects, trying to decide if I wanted to have a new home built.

I sat thinking about this dream and wondering what it was about.

Since I don't have a lot of time to delve into my dreams, I work on the titles and themes, hoping to get some clues. Each morning, after I write my dreams, I give them titles. Then I try to determine their themes.

I gave this dream the following title: "I am offered a very large book covered in plastic for my course." But this title alone did not relate to anything going on in my life.

When I got to the theme, it hit me with great clarity: *I have concerns about taking on more than I can handle or more than I want to deal with.* Do I really want to take on the enormous task of building a house, without really knowing what I am getting into?

The most common dream work method

Most of my early dream education involved reading books and taking workshops to learn some formal approaches to dream work so that I might more fully understand what my dreams were trying to say. The most common method of working with dreams is to involve oneself with dream symbols.

In the context of dream work, symbols are the images that appear in your dreams. They may be people, animals, animate or inanimate objects—even undefined blobs. They also may be the colors in the dream. They may be the words heard or imagined in your dream.

Dreams speak to you in symbolic language. Your task in working with the symbols is to attempt to decipher the language and see what meaning it might have in your life. The symbols that have the most significance and that spark our interest are those that evoke emotion.

For years, I have found great benefit in working with my dreams by investigating the symbolism. But I have become dissatisfied with working solely with this approach for several reasons.

- Evaluating the significance of a symbol in a dream can be tedious and time-consuming. Let's say you have a dream about a horse. What is a horse? Why is it the color it is? Is it a male or female? What does it mean to be male or female? Does that matter in this dream?

- To fully understand the significance of a symbol in a dream, you must first examine its context within the dream. What is this particular dream horse doing in this particular dream? What are the horse's surroundings? What are the feelings of the horse?

- Symbols can be misleading, depending on how you interpret their meaning. Why is this particular dream horse in this particular dream? Why is this horse acting the way it does?

- Dealing with the vast number of symbols or images in a dream multiplies the degree of effort and time needed to arrive at the message the dream is trying to convey. What about the other animals the horse is interacting with? What about the barn? The fence? The thunderstorm? People in the dream?

- Symbols do not have universal meanings that carry over from one dream to the next. You've had dreams of horses before and you think you understand what they mean to you. But does this horse have the same meaning in this dream? Maybe. Maybe not.

Dreams are striving to send a message. Seeking that message solely through symbolism can delay delivery of that message to our consciousness. Dream imagery and symbolism will vary considerably from night to night. But the major issue or message the dreams are trying to convey to you may repeat. For instance, in a three-dream sequence, one dream may be about riding a horse, the next about driving a car, and the next about moving furniture, but the recurring theme may deal with being out of control. If we miss the point based on misinterpretation of a particular symbol, we will get the message in another form. And we will keep getting that message in different forms—different imagery—until we get the point.

Getting back to my dream, if all I did was identify the title, I would have missed the important message it was trying to convey— the issue that I needed to deal with at the time. If I had just worked with the symbols, it would have taken me much longer to get to the core—the "heart"—of the dream. My real insight came from determining the theme. I did not have to wait for the message to come in different forms—different imagery—until I got the point.

It's time for a change of focus

I believe a new approach to dream work is needed. It requires a change of focus.

Thomas Moore, in his book *Care of the Soul*, best explains the philosophy behind the approach I propose. He says, "Storytelling . . . helps us see the themes that circle in our lives, the deep themes that tell the myths we live. It would take only a slight shift in emphasis . . . to focus on the storytelling itself rather than on its interpretations."[1]

Dreams are usually presented as stories. The storytelling form makes it easier for you to direct your focus on what is important for your health and well-being. But symbolic analysis of the dream places your concentration on *interpretation* rather than on the dream story. You are likely to get so caught up in trying to determine what the dream "means" that you might miss the point of the story. By working directly with the theme or themes of the dream—using methods I shall present in this book—you can simplify the dream evaluation process. These methods can also supplement symbolic representation work.

My introduction to themes

Much of the practical knowledge I have gained about working with dreams I learned from my good friend Rita Dwyer. Rita is a founding member and former president of the International Association for the Study of Dreams. In 1959, Rita's life was saved because of a dream. In the aerospace lab where she was working at the time, a fellow worker pulled her out of a fire caused when an experiment she was working on exploded in her face. He reacted automatically, performing actions he had done repeatedly in a recurring dream. Because of that event, Rita has devoted her life to educating others about the value of dreams.

Rita has conducted numerous dream workshops throughout the world. She created the D.C. Area Dream Community in northern Virginia—a place where people could gather once or twice a month to discuss their dreams. In one of these sessions, Rita introduced me to a dream work technique that she found in the book *Dreams and Spiritual Growth* by Louis M. Savary, Patricia H. Berne, and Strephon Kaplan Williams. This technique is called TTAQ, which stands for Title, Theme, Affect, and Question. The authors suggest you give each dream a Title, determine the Theme, and note the dream Affect—the feelings or emotions that were generated by the dream. The Question you need to ask in this technique is not what question the dream answers, but what question the dream asks.

In my attempts to teach the TTAQ technique to workshop participants, I have found that the most difficult part of the process for them was determining the theme of the dream. I looked for advice on this in the current dream literature and found it sorely lacking.

With so many dream books on the market, does the world really need another book about dreams?

There are many excellent books available that offer advice on such dream work methods as titling, interpreting symbols, drawing your dreams, turning them into poems, and so on. Relatively few deal directly with dream themes. The best of the books related to themes include Gayle Delaney's *In Your Dreams*, a collection of the most common themes she has discovered in her experience, and Patricia Garfield's book *The Universal Dream Key*, describing twelve common dream themes found throughout the world. Some examples of common themes found in both books include falling and flying, being chased, and being naked in public. Both authors include methods for relating these common themes to your personal dreams and applying them to your life.

I believe that what Delaney and Garfield define as common themes are actually "dream activity" for which the specific messages, ideas, or perceptions—the inherent themes—are yet to be defined.

For example, one of the most common dreams experienced by humanity is being naked in public. I asked myself, "What is the core theme of this dream activity?" After some introspection, I realized that dreams of being naked—or even well dressed—in public relate to self-identity and one's outlook on life. Self-identity is a common theme for which the "being naked in public" dream is but one example.

I have yet to find a book that gives dreamers detailed instructions on how to determine and work with the themes of their own dreams. Existing books on dream work do not address methods of defining dream themes. And they do not provide a means of identifying actual common themes you can relate to your dreams.

My intent with this book is to fill these missing gaps.

What this book is about

This book presents a new approach to working with dreams. It specifically addresses the themes presented in dream life and their relationship to waking life.

This is a how-to book. You will learn how to identify the themes in your dreams and how to use them as tools for living in the waking world.

If working with dreams is new to you, this book offers suggestions on recording, reviewing, and interacting with your dreams and integrating the messages they offer into your life. If you have been working with dreams for some time, this book introduces the concept of themes and shows you how to incorporate them into personal dream work processes with which you may already be familiar.

What are themes?

The "heart" of anything is generally accepted as the central, most vital part. It is the center of your being. It is the place where the deepest emotions and sensibilities are felt. It is that place within your personality where soul essence resides. Dreams come from this center. Your dreams are trying to awaken you to your soul purpose, your soul essence. The dream theme is the vital message coming from this place, filled with all the emotion that will spur you on to new discoveries and a higher level of awareness about yourself and what you need to grow and develop.

The theme of a dream is that important message, idea, or perception that the dream is attempting to bring to your conscious mind. The theme gets right to the core of what your dream is trying to say.

What themes are not

Themes are not story plots. As you read a novel or watch a movie, you follow the plot and begin to get an idea of the basic message the author was trying to convey. You may have heard that there is some finite number of basic themes in movies and literature. The Internet Public Library (http://www.ipl.org) reports that there are various numbers of plots in literature. These are not themes. However, one common theme emerges within all the plots—conflict. One way to best explain a situation is to present its inherent conflicts—its oppositions, its disharmonies. In this polarized world in which we live, our lives are built on such conflicts: right/wrong, he/she, Republican/Democrat, and so on.

This may be true in dreams, as well. In dreams, the plots are the actions taking place around the symbolic imagery. They may suggest conflict. They certainly evoke emotion. They stir us to seek out the message—the theme—being conveyed. Themes are not plots.

Themes are also differentiated from types of movies and books. There are adventure epics, love stories, sci-fi creations, war remembrances, and horror stories. These are different types of stories that could have common themes or ideas or messages. For instance, the theme of good versus evil, as well as other examples of human conflict, could be found in any one of these types of stories.

Authors of dream books will describe many types of dreams. They include, but are not limited to, the following: nightmares, lucid dreams, numinous dreams, precognitive dreams, telepathic dreams, and healing dreams. Each of these is distinguished *not* by the theme or message of the dream, but by the method through which the dream speaks to you.

Nightmares present you with dramatic messages, waking you up in terror or fear. Lucid dreams—dreams in which you are aware you are dreaming—allow you to consciously interact with the dream imagery, as if awake. Numinous dreams impart supernatural or spiritual messages, often presented as emotion or feeling rather than a story line. Precognitive dreams speak to you of possible future events. Telepathic dreams connect you with another person you may or may not know in waking life. Healing dreams present you with information about the condition of your body or psyche and offer suggestions for healing.

A single message or theme may be presented to you by each one of these dream types. Some believe a nightmare occurs when you have ignored or missed the point when the message was presented in other, more subtle ways.

Again, the theme of a dream is that important message, idea, or perception that the dream is attempting to bring to your conscious mind. The theme gets right to the heart of what your dream is trying to say. This same message could be presented under many different plots and through many different types of dreams.

What is the Theme Matrix?

The basic issues of life and of dreams can be described in terms of twelve distinct themes. These twelve themes are presented in this book in the form of a matrix.

A matrix is an arrangement of bits of information ordered in some logical fashion to be useful for determining relationships with other bits of information. In mathematics, the matrix is used to display quantities. In the computer industry, the matrix is an arrangement of memory elements. For our purposes in relation to dreams, the theme matrix is a listing of twelve core themes designed to help you relate the themes of your personal dreams to a set of common themes. You will also find the matrix helpful in working with events that arise in your waking life.

Why twelve?

This book describes the twelve core themes encompassing all activity in your dream life or waking life. It also includes a twelve-step process for working with your dreams. Why twelve?

There is significance in numbers. A prime example is the particular significance found in the number twelve.

Throughout history, twelve has been significant to humanity. All the world's great religions have the number twelve in their foundation, such as the twelve Disciples in Christianity. Whole nations have divided their tribes and their territories based on the number twelve. This concept was adopted in ancient Egypt, Phoenicia, Chaldaea, Persia, Babylonia, the Roman Empire, Greece, Gaul, Scandinavia, India, Tibet, Israel, Japan, China, Peru, Iceland, Africa, Madagascar, Polynesia, and many others.[2] Even today, we see the twelve nations of the Commonwealth of Independent States—the former U.S.S.R. Our days and nights are divided into twelve hours. Our years are divided into twelve months. There are twelve inches in a linear foot. Our juries consist of twelve members. These are just a few examples. (See Appendix B for further examples.)

The importance of the number twelve had its basis in astronomy. The ancient Sumerians are believed to have been the first to divide the heavens into twelve constellations, each identified by a distinctive sign or symbolic representation. For instance, the Sumerians called the first sign "field dweller," the second "heavenly bull," and so on. They believed that everything in human affairs was influenced by the effects of the constellations. The study of this phenomenon became a science called astrology. The Greeks called this astrological model of twelve constellations the zodiac. They assigned names of their gods to each of the constellations—Aries, Taurus, and so on.

According to astrologers, each sign of the zodiac represents specific characteristics. Persons born at the time one of the constellations was prominent in the heavens are believed to be under the influence of that constellation and may thus display some of the characteristics represented by that constellation. The characteristics of the signs of the zodiac have stood the test of time. Each sign of the zodiac can be described by a specific characteristic exerting a specific influence.

The characteristics of each sign also reflect a developmental progression. That is, the influence of each phase of the zodiac prepares us for the next phase. The zodiac is then a symbol for the life cycle. For our purposes, the term *life cycle* refers to all the developmental phases through which you progress in each aspect of your life. You live through many life cycles. The life cycle of a career. The life cycle of a relationship. The life cycle of education. The life cycle of a specific project.

The meaningful cycles in your life—in fact, all cycles of nature— can be explained in terms of twelve phases corresponding to the zodiacal sequence. For instance, the original meanings of the twelve constellations in Chinese astrology correspond to the twelve stages of the yearly life cycle of the cereal plant. If you read these as taking place in the twelve months of the year, beginning in January, the life cycle becomes clear: "(1) seed, roots; (2) swelling, taking in water; (3) opening, coming out; (4) birth; (5) standing up; (6) fruits; (7) delicious (ripe fruits); (8) colorful; (9) taking in, harvest; (10) appreciate, sorting harvest; (11) choosing (new seeds); and (12) storing (dormancy)."[3]

The life cycles in nature also correspond to the zodiacal sequence in modern Western astrology. Dane Rudhyar, one of the world's most prolific and respected astrologers, presents the same correspondence of the twelve constellations to the seasons. Rudhyar describes the spring-summer half of the year cycle as a time of individualizing, and the fall-winter half is a time of collectivization. He further divides the year into four periods. Spring is the time of differentiation, corresponding to the time of new birth and opening up. Summer is the time of stabilization, relating to the time when the fruits emerge and ripen and when flowers bloom in full color. Fall is the time of group integration, the time of harvest and choosing new seeds. Winter is the time of capitalization, when we store our food and begin planting and nurturing new seeds for spring growth. Rudhyar says that these four seasons correspond "generally with the four basic periods of any cycle of cosmic manifestation, whether micro- or macrocosmic."[4]

We have all the elements of nature within us. Therefore, we also have the rhythm of twelve ingrained in us. The Theme Matrix presented in this book is based primarily on the cyclical rhythm of twelve as reflected in the twelve zodiacal influences.

The life cycle is a spiral. As you progress through phases in the life cycle and feel you have completed the cycle, it seems as if you have returned to the beginning to start a new cycle. But you do not return to where you started; you never regress. You begin the cycle again at a higher level of understanding. You are always progressing forward. Cycles repeat, but events never repeat exactly as they happened before. You always enter into a new cyclic phase with a higher level of consciousness and awareness.

How this book will help you

This book shows you how to work with the themes of your dreams and your life experiences for personal understanding and growth. The first three chapters give you the basics for exploring the underlying issues being brought to your consciousness. Chapter 4 provides guidance on how to grow and benefit from this newly acquired self-knowledge.

Chapter 1 provides detailed guidance on what themes are and how to determine them—not just for dreams, but for any event in your life.

Chapter 2 introduces the Theme Matrix and provides detailed guidance on how to work with it. The matrix offers descriptions of twelve broad themes that will help you to determine on what area of your life your dreams or waking-life experiences are inviting you to focus. The matrix can also help you determine where you are in the life cycle of that area of focus and help you move on to the next step in the cycle.

Chapter 3 shows you how to incorporate themes and the Theme Matrix into your daily dream work. This chapter presents twelve processes or steps that will help you work with your dreams.

Chapter 4 provides guidance on how to benefit from the "theme" work you have done. Again working with the twelve core themes in the Theme Matrix, you will learn how to deal with the issues raised in your dreams by taking positive action in your waking life. This is called "honoring" the dream.

The twelve theme descriptions in chapter 2 and the twelve dream work processes in chapter 3 are presented in the context of the four major life cycle sequences described above. For our purposes, we will use the terms differentiation, expression, interaction, and capitalization as the four parts or phases of the life cycle.

This book is intended to help you understand and grow through your own life cycles.

Through differentiation and expression, you come to understand yourself as an individual. Through interaction and capitalization, you come to understand yourself as a member of society and the world community.

Focusing on how you differentiate yourself as an individual prepares you to learn self-expression. Focusing on how you express yourself prepares you to learn how to interact with others—first one, then many. Focusing on how you interact with others prepares you to learn to serve the whole of humanity. Focusing on the whole of humanity prepares you to begin to redifferentiate yourself as an individual at a higher level of consciousness. The cycle continues.

one

Identifying and Determining Themes

*The real voyage of discovery
consists not in seeking new
landscapes, but in having new eyes.*

——MARCEL PROUST

This chapter provides detailed guidance on what themes are and how to determine them. You can use the methods shown in this chapter to help you identify and express themes in any context.

In the twelve-step process of dream work to follow in chapter 3, you are encouraged to determine themes for your waking-life experiences as well as your dreams. This chapter will provide you with the information needed to do this.

Ingredients of a theme

We defined themes in the introduction, specifically in relation to dreams. We learned that they are not story plots or types of stories. They are related more to the underlying message a story or event is presenting to us. The best way to define themes is to examine the event itself.

Any event, be it a waking-life experience, a book, a movie, or a dream, has two basic ingredients. It has one or more characters, and it has activity.

Characters are defined here in the broadest sense. They may be people, animals, or inanimate objects. They often are just you, the observer. For instance, when you experience a beautiful sunset, the only "characters" present may be you and the sun. When you catch the scent of aromatic flowers, the only "characters" present are you and the flowers. Yet each of these events includes two basic ingredients: a character or characters and the event of sharing beauty through sight or smell.

Each activity in which we engage serves some purpose. Experiencing the aroma of flowers may be solely for the purpose of momentary pleasure or enjoyment.

Every event broadens our consciousness and awakens us to new understanding. The flowers we experience today have never before been in the world the way they are now and never will be again.

Every event affects our attitudes about what we like and dislike in our world. We learn that some flowers are more attractive to us than others and smell better than others.

Every event presents us with decisions we can choose to make about how to move on from this experience. We can decide to avoid the flowers that we find distasteful and surround ourselves with those we find pleasurable.

Each activity in which the characters in our lives engage serves a purpose. It brings us to new awareness. The way to realize that purpose is to seek out the core message in the experience. This core message is the theme of that event.

The theme of any event you experience is that important message, idea, or perception that the event is attempting to bring to your conscious mind.

That core message, idea, or perception may come to you through interaction with your friends. It may come from watching total strangers interact. It may come from a book you read or a movie you see. Or it may come from a dream.

The theme of a dream is that important message, idea, or perception that the dream is attempting to bring to your conscious mind. The theme gets to the heart of what your dream is trying to say. Also, if you view your waking life as a dream, you can learn from the messages, ideas, or perceptions presented to you by your experiences. Determining the themes of your dreams and the themes of your waking-life experiences places the important issues of your life on the front burner so you can face them and deal with them intelligently. Following are the methods you can use to evaluate any experience and determine its theme.

How to determine themes

Determining the theme of an event essentially involves observing the actions of the main character—or interactions of multiple characters—and identifying the essential point of the activity or the reason for the activity. You can facilitate this process by asking yourself these questions:

(1) What basic activity is going on? (The action itself may be the theme.)

(2) What is the major issue concerning the characters? (The issue being dealt with may be the theme.)

(3) What is the apparent or presumed motivation of the characters that causes them to act in this way? What drives the characters' behavior? Is it emotion? Is it an innate characteristic of the main character or characters? Is it the attitude the character or characters have about the main issue?

For example, let's consider the following event, which could be a dream or something you might actually face in waking life. (Let's hope it is the former.)

You are camping. A bear comes along. You run away.

Here are some suggested responses to the three basic questions that can lead us to a theme for this event:

(1) What basic activity is going on? This event involves two characters: you and the bear. You have certain plans that concern personal enjoyment. You do not necessarily plan involvement with others, especially not someone or something larger and more threatening than yourself. But you may consider this situation one in which you are overpowered and threatened. From the standpoint of your actions alone, you might consider a theme such as *I have gotten myself into a situation I did not anticipate.* From the standpoint of the interactions of the characters, you might say the theme is *I am being overpowered by something larger or stronger than myself.*

(2) What is the major issue concerning the characters? From the standpoint of each character, the bear and the person running away, the issue is that of two characters being in the same space at the same time, neither of whom may be particularly happy with the presence of the other. The theme in this case might be *A confrontation occurs between two who are not used to being together*, or *A situation of potential conflict occurs.*

(3) What is the motivation of the characters? From the statement of the event as given, we can only surmise about motivation. For instance, we don't know if you were being chased away by the bear or if you just ran in anticipation of being

chased. Why did you not choose to scare the bear away? Or to fight back in some way?

All motivation can be described in terms of three types of energy: sensitivity, will, and intelligence.[5] When considering the prime motivation of characters, think in terms of these three broad categories.

- **Sensitivity.** This category is motivation based on caring, compassion, love, or applied wisdom. Examples include expressions of unconditional love, caring and compassion, strong feeling and emotion, working in partnership, and using wisdom gained to help others.

- **Will.** This category is motivation based on purpose, determination, or manifestations of power. Examples include using personal power and energy to meet challenges and fulfill personal visions, and expressing will to fulfill personal and shared desires.

- **Intelligence.** This category is motivation based on thought, reason, and adaptability. Examples include dealing with and adapting to opportunities missed or fulfilled, analyzing, strategizing, communicating, and accepting responsibility.

Emotion can be a strong motivator. In the event with the bear, did you react purely from emotion? If so, the emotion of fear may be the driving force in this event. An emotion can be a theme. Stated as a theme based on emotion, you might say *I am in fear of being overpowered*, or *I react based on fear*.

Exerting personal will—seeking to fulfill desire—is another prime motivator. A possible theme reflecting will and desire may be *I am in a life-and-death situation, and I choose life.*

Using your innate intelligence by applying thought and reason is the third prime motivator. In this event, did you logically consider the options and decide some other place was the safest place to be? In this case, you might say the theme is *I am under threat of being hurt,* or *I am avoiding pain,* or *I am running away from danger.* If you think of motivation from the standpoint of the bear, you might say *I am attempting to meet my basic survival needs.*

These are all suggestions on ways to look at events and determine their core messages, their underlying themes. These questions—these ways of looking at an event—can help you determine the essential points of the event and the reasoning behind the activity. You need to decide for yourself which one is most appropriate for each event. As you examine each event, ask yourself what aspect provides the most impact for you. Is it the action going on between the characters? Is it the dynamics of the issues involved? Or is it what motivates the characters to act as they do, based on their emotion, will, or reasoning?

How to word themes

There is no rule as to the best way to state a theme. Themes can be stated as full sentences or as a single word. They can be stated as a question. For instance, the recommended theme, *I am in fear of being overpowered,* is a full sentence. You may choose to word it *Being overpowered,* or just *Overpowered.* Or you may choose to state it as a question: *Am I being overpowered?*

The theme *A situation of potential conflict occurs* may also be worded *I am in a situation of potential conflict.* Or simply, *Potential conflict.* Stated as a question, it would be: *Am I in a situation involving potential conflict?*

In this discussion on determining themes, suggested themes were offered. Under close examination, they can be seen to have three basic characteristics. First, they are all personalized. Most of them begin with "I." Second, they are all written in the present tense, as if they were happening right now. For instance, most of them begin with "I am," rather than "I was." Third, rarely are words used in the theme statement that were used in defining the event itself. Following are suggested guidelines for wording themes using these three basic characteristics.

(1) Personalizing is the first basic characteristic of wording the theme.

When attempting to identify and determine themes, characters in an event can be anything. They are not just people. They can be inanimate objects or animals. This is because everything in our experience can be said to characterize some quality or energy. Many of our common expressions emphasize this: eats like a bird . . . a real wolf . . . peace dove . . . something's fishy . . . latest flame . . . I'm floored . . . in a fog . . . ghost of a chance . . . good as gold.

Identifying with the object—personalizing it—by calling the object "me" allows you to see the quality or energy that you associate with that object as an aspect of yourself. You can ask yourself why this object is being presented to you at this time. And why in this context? Is this a quality that you need to be working with?

An example of an action character that we normally think of as an inanimate object is a car. Cars are extremely common in dreams. Many times themes can jump right out at you by examining the action of a dream car. Personalizing the car makes this even easier to see. Consider the following car-related themes. What is the impact to you when you see the word "I" or "me" included? *What is driving me? I am in control. I am out of control. I am being chased. I am being transported. I am being protected from harm.*

It is not important to focus on what an action character does in general, but rather what *this particular* character is doing in *this particular* situation—this waking-life event or this dream.

(2) The second important characteristic of wording themes is to word them in the present tense.

In fact, it is also best to relate the event itself as if it were happening now, in the present. Why is this?

It is common to discuss an event or dream in the past tense. After all, it was something that happened in the past. But when we talk about it as a past event, we are less likely to own it and take responsibility for it as something we need to deal with right now. We are more likely to brush it under the table as something we don't have to face. Often these events and dreams are presenting something to us that needs to come to consciousness. By stating them as if they are happening at this moment, we are more open to experience all the dynamics and emotions that accompany the events.

By stating a theme in the present tense, such as *I am out of control*, you can feel and accept the intensity of the message being presented. Stating it in the past tense, *I was out of control*, lessens the impact and allows you to imply to yourself that this is no longer an issue you need to face.

(3) The third characteristic of theme writing is to avoid using the words and specific actions from the event or dream.

This characteristic is perhaps the most important. If you were to adapt rules for your theme writing, this would be the cardinal rule.

Themes are not always easy to determine. Therefore, our natural tendency is to simply restate the actions of the event. For instance, in the case of being chased across a mountain by a bear, your natural impulse might be to say the theme is *Being chased*. But considering your emotional state during this event, the theme is more likely *Fear of being overpowered*. The theme based on the major issue at hand might be *Under threat of being hurt*. Your motivation is "avoiding pain." Each of these statements avoids using the actual words and actions of the event.

By making it a rule to seek out new words and actions in determining a theme, you force yourself to get at the message the event is presenting to you. You get to its core—to the heart of the event.

Another example of this is a dream in which you are unable to lace your shoes. The title might simply be "Unable to lace my shoes," whereas the theme would be *I can't do a simple task*.

Themes can be stated as full sentences, in a word or a few words, or as a question. Understanding themes comes easiest when they are personalized, stated in the present tense, and are not just reiterations of the words or actions in the event.

Complex events and dreams

When you begin this task of investigating events and dreams in depth, you will soon realize that an event may appear to have more than one theme. Individual events and dreams may involve many different types of activities. Many are like plays with different acts, often involving different characters and locales. So it is likely that in a specific event or dream you may feel there is more than one message or idea or concept being presented. How can you deal with this? Is it still possible to find a single, primary core theme?

The key to examining any event or dream with multiple "acts"— or other indications suggesting multiple themes—is to look for commonalities in the actions, issues, and motivations of the characters. There may be several messages being presented, but it is likely that there is a single core theme. The best way to explain this is with an example.

The following is a summary of a long dream. Note that it is told in the first person and in the present tense.

> I am heading toward a new assignment, a new place I have been assigned to work. I feel it is quite prestigious. I am dressed quite casually and have the feeling they will expect me to wear a business suit and tie. I am not looking forward to that and expect I will debate it with them. I get close to where I think this place is. I am in a large building. I go to a large central area where they are preparing a ceremony with flags. I think they are going to honor someone. I almost get in the way and have to go around things and people to get through. I go down a hallway to the right. I look in rooms as I go by. I eventually go in but seem to find myself on something like an outdoor train platform. A man asks me what I want or what I am looking for. I tell him I am reporting for a position here. At first he asks if I wouldn't rather go freshen up or check in to where I am staying. But I know I only have a small bag with me. I really have very little and am still concerned they will not be happy that I am not dressed more formally.

Two distinct issues are apparent here. One can be stated as the following theme: *I am searching for my place.* Another has to do with not feeling properly dressed: *I am concerned about my self-image,* or *I am concerned about how I present myself.* Where can we find commonalities in these statements? The actions have to do with the dreamer's drive to find a place in the world where he or she can serve and produce a livelihood. They also reveal a motivation to fit in with society. These are both important life issues. With this in mind, a core theme might be *I am seeking worthiness and acceptance.*

This example shows how you can link the common threads of a dream or event together. The result is a characteristic or issue you can now relate to your waking life.

Can you see similarities in the next dream example to the one we just examined?

> I am with one other person, a man. We go into an
> enormous building that takes up a whole city block.
> It is some sort of organization, perhaps humanitarian.
> People there tell us we are free to wander in any direc-
> tion. I look up a short flight of stairs and can see into a
> room. I see it is a kitchen. I look to the right to a flight
> of stairs that goes down. I know or am told this goes to
> the boiler room. I'm surprised they want us to feel free
> to investigate their whole operation. We go to a room
> farther down on this side of the building. At some point
> I am shown a large room with a cashier at one end. I am
> not really there but see it somehow. I am left alone as
> the other man goes off to collect money. I may have
> been invited to collect money as well. At any rate, I de-
> cide to try it. I grab a little bag of money and begin to
> wander through this place. I pass people, but I know
> that I am not good at asking people to give, so I just
> keep wandering.

Here again, we can see two distinct activities involving this dream character. The first is wandering in new space. The second is a feeling of inadequacy about asking people to give money. The dream character in the example before this one was also wandering, but for a different purpose: he or she was motivated toward a specific goal. We don't know what the specific motivation of this dream character is. Perhaps just curiosity.

In both dreams, the primary dream character has concerns about personal limitations or inadequacy. Whereas in the earlier dream the character was seeking a way to improve in this area, in this dream he or she continues wandering without motivation to improve, perhaps as a means of avoidance of the issue. This suggests the following possible theme: *I explore new spaces as a way to avoid dealing with my limitations and feelings of inadequacy.* It offers a message that can be of value to the dreamer.

This gives you several ideas of how to work with multiple activities within a dream. It is important to look for commonalities in the activities, issues, and motivations of the characters.

The two themes just discussed may remind you of waking-life events that you might have experienced. A good example of the first theme is a job interview. When you are seeking employment, you face a multitude of feelings. You have expectations of what bosses or personnel officers think about how you should dress. You are not sure if this is the right job for you; you perhaps are just "searching for your place." But you want to make the best impression possible, so you make sure you are on time and attempt to present yourself in the best possible light. You know you can do the job, but you need to convince someone else of that. The theme of the job interview might be the same as the first dream example: *I am seeking worthiness and acceptance.* Someone who is shy or insecure on a new job may offer a good example of the second theme. He or she may allow the mind to "wander" aimlessly to avoid dealing with the new situation. The same theme may apply: *I explore new spaces as a way to avoid dealing with my limitations and feelings of inadequacy.* The issue he or she needs to deal with is to accept those limitations and become willing to seek improvement.

Personal theme exercise

At this point, you are encouraged to examine some dreams or waking-life experiences of your own. Select a recent event or dream of your own that you have been curious about. Perhaps you are wondering if it deals with a waking-life issue you need to face. Perhaps you just want to understand it a little better. Get to the core message, idea, or perception of this event by determining its theme.

Take out a notebook or a blank piece of paper. Write a brief statement of the event or dream. Be sure to write it in the present tense, as if it were happening right now.

Ask yourself the following questions:

- What is the basic activity going on in this event?

- What issue or issues are being presented?

- What is the motivation of the characters?
  - Is it based on sensitivity, love, caring, compassion, or applied wisdom?
  - Is it based on will, desire, purpose, determination, or power considerations?
  - Is it based on thought, logic, reasoning, or the need to adapt to a situation?

Write a personalized theme, in the present tense, avoiding the specific words or actions in the event itself. It may be written as a full sentence, a brief phrase, or as a question.

If you are having trouble coming up with a dream or current life experience of your own to work on, try this one:

I am on a bus, apparently going home. It is late and dark out. I see my hotel coming up on the right. I wonder if the bus has those pull cords so I can try to get the driver to stop for me. I find one just as we are passing the place. I pull it. But the driver says something I can't hear. I get the impression he is saying that he can't stop here. I hear him say something about stopping at the gas station up on the corner. I see us pull into town. I'm concerned about walking back to the hotel on the road in the dark. I think one or two of the others say they will walk back with me. I feel support from others.

What is the theme of this dream? Is there more than one activity going on? If so, can you determine a common core theme?

———

In this chapter we have examined themes—what they are and how to determine them in any context. In summary, we covered the following points:

- Themes allow you to explore any event or dream. They help you identify that important message, idea, or perception that the event or dream is attempting to bring to your conscious mind.

- We can determine themes by examining the actions, issues, and motivations of the characters.

- Themes are best understood when you personalize them—that is, when you can associate the characters and objects as aspects of yourself.

- You are encouraged to state themes in the present tense, avoiding use of the specific words or actions in the event or dream.

You now have the basics for working with themes so that you can incorporate them into your daily dream work. Themes are a key ingredient in the twelve-step process of dream work to follow in chapter 3.

two

The Theme Matrix

It's the question that drives us.

—CARRIE-ANNE MOSS AS
TRINITY, *The Matrix*

Ingredients of the Theme Matrix

A matrix is an arrangement of bits of information ordered in some logical fashion to be useful for determining relationships with other bits of information. In mathematics, the matrix is used to display quantities. In the computer industry, the matrix is an arrangement of memory elements.

The Theme Matrix is a listing of twelve theme categories designed to help you relate the themes of your personal dreams and your life issues to a common set of themes.

Think of this as a model containing twelve universally accepted messages, ideas, or perceptions that you can use to evaluate and explore the themes of your dream life and your waking life. The basic issues and concerns of life and of dreams can be described in terms of these twelve distinct themes. The Theme Matrix has been drawn from many sources. It is largely based on the houses in astrology but also draws from archetypal references, common dreams experienced throughout the world, and life experience.

The matrix describes twelve distinct groupings of human activity—twelve basic life activities or themes. The matrix is intended to offer you a deeper understanding of the themes you will encounter in your dreams and waking life.

The themes of your dreams and waking-life activities may come to you as positive or negative experiences. For instance, the fact that you are being chased in a dream is normally seen as a negative and scary thing. But you may see pursuit by a lover as a positive experience.

World-renowned dream explorer Jeremy Taylor's first basic assumption about dreams is that "All dreams come in the service of health and wholeness"[6]—even the dark, nasty ones. Perhaps a dream with a common theme presented in both its positive and negative forms may be coming to offer the same message. The reason it comes as "dark" or "light" may be a function of the degree to which we have accepted a message in our consciousness and have been willing to explore it or work with it.

For example, we said earlier that a common dream activity is being naked in public. This is normally seen as a negative dream. However, if being dressed in a dream is of significance to the dreamer, this could be seen as positive. What would a common theme be for being naked or dressed in public? Looking at the theme in both its negative and positive senses, the dreamer is concerned about how he or she appears to others. In both cases, there is concern about personal image. In both cases, the dreamer is looking at self-acceptance. A common theme might be stated as: *How I feel about myself and how I present myself to others.* A dream in which you are embarrassed at being naked in front of other people might indicate that you are dealing with issues in your waking life about your self-image and self-acceptance. On the other hand, your dream of self-satisfaction at being immaculately dressed at a formal function might indicate the same thing. The negative dream is more likely to spur you into action about your issues, whereas the positive dream may reveal acceptance that what you are doing socially is right at this time.

The common core themes in the Theme Matrix represent the twelve activities—aspects of life, instinctive forces, underlying life principles, and lessons of life—that are common throughout humanity. They can help one address the positive or negative side of any issue or concern. And they can be used to represent the twelve key phases in any cyclical life journey.

Why are the core themes expressed as questions?

The twelve common core themes are expressed in the Theme Matrix as questions.

It is human nature for us to want answers to our problems and life concerns. But we seem to be faced with unending questions. This is true with dreams as well. Dreams appear to present more questions than they do answers. Even after a thorough examination of dreams, they seem to leave us with a new question. They leave us with a sense of mystery.

Caroline Myss says, "What if the mystery was the answer to your question? What if the journey toward getting to know divinity was to enter into mystery, to leave allegiance to human order and your need to have things explained in human logical fashion? The more confusing a situation is, the more the hand of God is there."[7] It is the mystery, the open-ended adventure expressed in the question, that motivates you and helps you to grow.

The mystery—the question that has not yet been fully examined by you—is expressed in the theme of your dream. The theme shows you the aspect of your life that you need to be dealing with at this moment. It shows you in what area of your life you need to be asking questions of yourself.

Years ago there was a television show called "Twenty Questions." So-called experts were allowed to ask up to twenty questions of a guest to see if they could determine his or her occupation. The model for working with dream themes presented in this book asks twelve questions that can help you determine what your "occupation" is at the moment. That is, what is occupying your mind? Your emotions? Your physical state? Your will or purpose? Armed with this information, you are then able to seek ways of dealing with your questions—your current issues and concerns.

With this concept in mind, the definition of dream themes could also be stated as follows: *The themes of a dream are the questions the dream is asking you to pursue for the benefit of your health and wholeness at this moment in your life.*

The twelve core themes of the Theme Matrix are statements of the twelve basic issues and concerns faced daily by all human beings. The fact that they appear in our dreams indicates that they are occupying our minds at some level—consciously or unconsciously. The very fact that we consider them to be issues and concerns means they are questions yet unanswered. They are a mystery.

It is the mystery, the open-ended adventure expressed in the question, that drives us. Motivates us. Helps us to grow.

The twelve core themes, expressed as questions

Following is a listing of the twelve core themes in the Theme Matrix. They are written as questions you can ask yourself to help you understand and work with your current issues and the various journeys of your life.

The twelve core themes are divided into four types of general activity, as they represent the four life cycles in all life activity: differentiation, expression, interaction, and capitalization. These too are presented as questions you can ask yourself regarding the issue you are facing. Each general activity includes three core themes.

Below each core theme are three distinct aspects or fields of activity that are pertinent to this theme. The negative and positive aspects of each theme are identified in the Theme Matrix under a single theme statement. A generalization of these opposing aspects is indicated after each theme statement.

How do you differentiate yourself from others?

Core theme #1. What is your personal self-image? Who are you?

Opposing aspects: self-acceptance/nonacceptance

- Self-identity—your perception about how you look and appear before the world.

- Outlook on life—your expectations about being accepted by others and the degree to which you feel accepted by others.

- Vulnerability—susceptibility to being injured, attacked, or criticized. Your feelings of vulnerability lead you to seek physical, emotional, and mental safety and protection.

Core theme #2. What personal resources do you have and need for security and self-reliance?

Opposing aspects: needs satisfied/needs not satisfied

- Possessions—your material possessions, capabilities, and financial resources.

- Self-reliance—the ability to provide for yourself, physically and emotionally.

- Power and energy—the strength and endurance needed to control your actions.

Core theme #3. How do you synthesize and communicate personal thought?

Opposing aspects: functioning well/not functioning well

- Thinking—your ability to reason and synthesize thought, enabling you to function in your environment.

- Environment—your day-to-day world, the circumstances you face, and your intellectual capabilities.

- Communication—your ability to organize and express your thoughts.

How do you express yourself or learn self-expression?

Core theme #4. How do you express your feelings and compassion and develop a sense of "home"?

Opposing aspects: being nurtured/needing care

- Feeling—how you express your feelings and how feelings affect you.

- Nurturing—how you "mother," or watch over and nourish, others and yourself.

- Home base—a place or mental state that provides stability for you.

Core theme #5. How do you exert your will so that you may express creativity, explore, and discover?

Opposing aspects: unlimited opportunity/limited opportunity

- Creativity—how you express your innate personal creativity and how you remove limitations that inhibit your creativity.

- Will—deciding what you want and choosing courses of action to get you there.

- Romance—learning about what you love and seeking ways to express that love while still holding on to your independence and will.

Core theme #6. How do you use your analytical skills to develop confidence to meet challenges?

Opposing aspects: success/failure

- Self-confidence—assurance within yourself that you have potential and all the analytical skills you need to adapt and meet the challenges of life.

- Challenges—the tests that life gives you; crises and conflicts that build self-confidence and prepare you to interact with and help others.

- Service—applying your skills and abilities in meaningful work.

How do you interact with others?

Core theme #7. How do you achieve balance and learn to love through a partner?

Opposing aspects: feeling loved/feeling threatened

- Partnership—making a commitment to a person, cause, field of work, or belief.

- Love—having intense affection for and wanting to be committed to someone or something you desire.

- Balance—seeking harmony with something or someone you love and with whom you are in partnership. It involves give and take.

Core theme #8. How do you let go of ego by sharing resources, yet still fulfill personal desires?

Opposing aspects: revived and healed/victimized

- Regeneration—death of the ego self and birth of the "true" self; finding your true identity, not influenced by family or upbringing.

- Joint resources—physical and interpersonal resources you share in your partnerships.

- Desire—your wishes and dreams; what you imagine your ideal world to be.

Core theme #9. How do you adapt or broaden your perspective through conceptualized thought?

Opposing aspects: mobility/immobility

- High consciousness—cognizance of the greater good for yourself and others; accepting responsibility for leading an ordered life.

- Perspective—openness and willingness to adapt to other viewpoints.

- Future orientation—planning and being open to potentialities and opportunities.

How do you capitalize on your experiences?

Core theme #10. How do you apply what you have learned from the past to benefit yourself and society?

Opposing aspects: gaining from experience or improving/failing to gain from experience or falling behind

- Achievement—recognition by yourself and others of what you have accomplished and learned from your past.

- Using—applying what you have learned to benefit yourself and society.

- Transformation—converting mental, emotional, and spiritual energy into physical form; changing the nature of your world by applying your wisdom in thought, word, and deed.

Core theme #11. What do you know to be truly essential and of value for yourself and society?

Opposing aspects: being guided and hopeful/being misled and fearful

- Community—collectivity; group identity; seeing your relationship with all of humanity.

- Truth—knowing what is essential and of value for yourself and humanity beyond what others say or what you read.

- Nonattachment—giving up attachments to petty illusions and desires.

Core theme #12. What do you believe about freeing yourself from boundaries and achieving wholeness?

Opposing aspects: unrestricted and in control/restricted or overwhelmed

- Duality—polarization; the struggle between two opposing tendencies or possibilities.

- Freedom—release from voluntary or involuntary confinements or restrictions.

- Wholeness—integration of the different aspects of yourself; also recognition of yourself as one with all life.

Finding your core theme in the Theme Matrix

The chart on pages 44–45 is a quick reference guide to the matrix. Use the following steps to find your core theme.

Step 1

Select a dream or waking-life event or activity that you wish to examine in greater detail. Choose one that sparks emotion within you or poses questions for you. As an aid in following the steps in this procedure, let's track the following dream:

> I am going down a trail with some others. We are walking alongside a wide river. The cliffs on both sides are getting higher and higher. I can see ahead around a bend. There is more snow on the cliff sides the farther along we are to go. It is quite beautiful and magnificent. The cliffs seem quite powerful. The trail seems to meander a bit. I feel some of the people are in conflict about how to proceed.

If this were your dream, you might choose it for study because of emotions you felt concerning the beauty and magnificence of the scenery. Or you might have questions about what this might have to do with conflicts in your waking life.

Step 2

Ask yourself what question the basic activity is "asking." One of the following four general questions or activities will apply. These are based on the concept that all life activity can be described in terms of the four life cycles or processes: differentiation, expression, interaction, and capitalization.

- How do you differentiate yourself from others?

- How do you develop self-expression for interaction with others?

- How do you interact with others?

- How are you benefiting from your experiences and realizations?

Considering the dream example we are following, look at each of these questions. First, does the dream deal with how you differentiate yourself from others? It does not seem to involve your self-image or your need for security or self-reliance. You seem to be in an exploratory mode, observing the landscape and the reactions of others. This may indicate some involvement with your thought processes, the third aspect of self-differentiation, but you are not synthesizing thought or really communicating with anyone. So it does not seem that this dream deals with self-differentiation.

Second, does the dream deal with your self-expression? You "feel" that the other dream characters are dealing with conflict regarding the direction they are taking. This indicates some level of self-expression, both from the standpoint of your feelings and from the expression of will on the part of the other dream characters. There is not an indication that the dream deals with the expression of anyone's analytical skills, although such expression may be called for.

Third, does the dream deal with interaction? You, as the primary dream character, don't appear to be interacting with anyone. The other characters are perhaps interacting, in that you feel they are in conflict with each other. But the dream seems to deal more with your feelings than actual interaction between the other characters.

Finally, does the dream deal with capitalization? Are any of the dream characters gaining from what they have learned about serving the "community"? It appears they are all in more of a "seeker" mode, not yet ready to interact or benefit.

It would seem that the dream is primarily dealing with a question of self-expression. How do you feel about what you are exploring? How do you feel about conflict? About being lost or not going in the right direction?

Step 3

Determine the apparent or presumed motivation of the character or characters. Remember, a character can be any animate or inanimate object. It can be a person. It can be a color. It can be a thought.

One of the three general questions below will apply. As we learned in chapter 1, these are based on the concept that all motivation can be described in terms of three types of energy: sensitivity, will, and intelligence.

- Is the activity motivated by sensitivity, caring, love, or applied wisdom?

- Is the activity motivated by will, determination, or manifestations of power?

- Is the activity motivated by thought, reason, or adaptability?

Again considering the dream example, how would you answer these questions? The main characters in the dream are you and some others traveling with you. You are apparently enjoying the trip and are in more of an observing mode. The strongest indication of motivation seems to come from the other characters. This is where polarities are emerging. This is where conflict is erupting. Their motivation is not coming from a point of sensitivity, nor from reason or adaptability. The primary motivational energy within the dream deals with expressions of conflicting personal wills.

Step 4

Using the Theme Matrix chart on pages 44–45, look down the activity column and across the motivation row to find the suggested core theme or issue for your event or dream. For example, assume you have a dream that you are naked in public and feel awkward or embarrassed. You, the main dream character, feel separate and apart from the other characters. You are not dressed as they are. You are not like them at this moment. This is an activity involving differentiation. You are not expressing or interacting or applying what you have learned from this. You are differentiating yourself from others. Your motivation is one of sensitivity. You are in a feeling, sensory mode, not yet expressing your will or power or using reasoning to get yourself out of this situation. The core theme or issue then would be #1: What is your personal self-image? Who are you?

In the dream example we are following, the activity deals with self-expression. The motivation of the characters deals with will and determination. By matching the activity column and the motivation row, we find that the core theme question is #5: How do you exert your will so that you may express creativity, explore, and discover?

Step 5

Examine the question and the suggested activities listed with the core theme you have found. Does this fit logically with your dream or event? Does it *feel* right to you?

Considering the dream example we are following, it is interesting to note that in the dream, you are exploring and discovering new beauty. These activities are consistent with the core theme of this dream.

Also, let's examine three different ways you, the dreamer, may behave in the "naked in public" dream. If you are embarrassed and

THE THEME MATRIX—THEMES #1–6		
Find your core theme/issue by relating basic activity (columns) to motivation (rows).		
	Activity: What question is the basic activity asking?	
	How do you differentiate yourself from others?	*How do you express yourself or learn self-expression?*
Is it based on sensitivity, caring, love, or applied wisdom?	1. *What is your personal self-image? Who are you?* Life issues/aspects/fields of activity: • Self-identity—your perception about how you look and appear before the world. • Outlook on life—your expectations about being accepted by others and the degree to which you feel accepted by others. • Vulnerability—susceptibility to being injured, attacked, or criticized. Your feelings of vulnerability lead you to seek physical, emotional, and mental safety and protection.	4. *How do you express your feelings and compassion and develop a sense of "home"?* Life issues/aspects/fields of activity: • Feeling—how you express your feelings and how feelings affect you. • Nurturing—how you "mother," or watch over and nourish, others and yourself. • Home base—a place or mental state that provides stability for you.
Is it based on will, determination, or use of power?	2. *What personal resources do you have and need for security and self-reliance?* Life issues/aspects/fields of activity: • Possessions—your material possessions, capabilities, and financial resources. • Self-reliance—the ability to provide for yourself, physically and emotionally. • Power and energy—the strength and endurance needed to control your actions.	5. *How do you exert your will so that you may express creativity, explore, and discover?* Life issues/aspects/fields of activity: • Creativity—how you express your innate personal creativity and how you remove limitations that inhibit your creativity. • Will—deciding what you want and choosing courses of action to get you there. • Romance—learning about what you love and seeking ways to express that love, while still holding on to your independence and will.
Is it based on thought, reason, or adaptability?	3. *How do you synthesize and communicate personal thought?* Life issues/aspects/fields of activity: • Thinking—your ability to reason and synthesize thought, enabling you to function in your environment. • Environment—your day-to-day world, the circumstances you face, and your intellectual capabilities. • Communication—your ability to organize and express your thoughts.	6. *How do you use your analytical skills to develop confidence to meet challenges?* Life issues/aspects/fields of activity: • Self-confidence—assurance within yourself that you have potential and all the analytical skills you need to adapt and meet the challenges of life. • Challenges—the tests that life gives you; crises and conflicts that build self-confidence and prepare you to interact with and help others. • Service—applying your skills and abilities in meaningful work.

Motivation: What is the apparent or presumed motivation of the characters?

		THE THEME MATRIX—THEMES #7–12	
		Find your core theme/issue by relating basic activity (columns) to motivation (rows).	
		Activity: What question is the basic activity asking?	
		How do you interact with others?	*How do you capitalize on your experience?*
Motivation: What is the apparent or presumed motivation of the characters?	Is it based on sensitivity, caring, love, or applied wisdom?	7. *How do you achieve balance and learn to love through a partner?* Life issues/aspects/fields of activity: • Partnership—making a commitment to a person, cause, field of work, or belief. • Love—having intense affection for and wanting to be committed to someone or something you desire. • Balance—seeking harmony with something or someone you love and with whom you are in partnership. It involves give and take.	10. *How do you apply what you have learned from the past to benefit yourself and society?* Life issues/aspects/fields of activity: • Achievement—recognition by yourself and others of what you have accomplished and learned from your past. • Using—applying what you have learned to benefit yourself and society. • Transformation—converting mental, emotional, and spiritual energy into physical form; changing the nature of your world by applying your wisdom in thought, word, and deed.
	Is it based on will, determination, or use of power?	8. *How do you let go of ego by sharing resources, yet still fulfill personal desires?* Life issues/aspects/fields of activity: • Regeneration—death of the ego self and birth of the "true" self; finding your true identity, not influenced by family or upbringing. • Joint resources—physical and interpersonal resources you share in your partnerships. • Desire—your wishes and dreams; what you imagine your ideal world to be.	11. *What do you know to be truly essential and of value for yourself and society?* Life issues/aspects/fields of activity: • Community—collectivity; group identity; seeing your relationship with all of humanity. • Truth—knowing what is essential and of value for yourself and humanity beyond what others say or what you read. • Nonattachment—giving up attachments to petty illusions and desires.
	Is it based on thought, reason, or adaptability?	9. *How do you adopt or broaden your perspective through conceptualized thought?* Life issues/aspects/fields of activity: • High consciousness—cognizance of the greater good for yourself and others; accepting responsibility for leading an ordered life. • Perspective—openness and willingness to adapt to other viewpoints. • Future orientation—planning and being open to potentialities and opportunities.	12. *What do you believe about freeing yourself from boundaries and achieving wholeness?* Life issues/aspects/fields of activity: • Duality—polarization; the struggle between two opposing tendencies or possibilities. • Freedom—release from voluntary or involuntary confinements or restrictions. • Wholeness—integration of the different aspects of yourself; also recognition of yourself as one with all life.

hiding, the core theme may have to do with how you present yourself in public—consistent with core theme #1. However, if you are able to will yourself invisible or put on some magical clothes in your dream, you are expressing willpower—consistent with core theme #2, self-reliance. If you take decisive action and go find clothes or find a place to hide, the theme may be consistent with core theme #3—using your personal thought processes. Through this exercise, you can see that, although we stated earlier that the "naked in public" dream is primarily an example of theme #1, it can be representative of other themes.

Step 6

The information you have gathered through this exercise can now be used for further study. Record your logic and the results of your study. Chapter 3 provides detailed information on working with your dreams. But you may also use many of the steps in chapter 3 to work with any event in your life.

For example, one of the key questions you will learn to explore in chapter 3 is, "Where in your life are you experiencing or living out this theme?" Assuming the example dream was yours, can you see where in your waking life you are in conflict about how to proceed? Or where you are headed?

The Theme Matrix at work

A member of our dream group in Black Mountain, North Carolina, told a dream in which she was watching an elegant, sensitive, handsome young Chinese man. She said it felt like she was watching a play. In the "play," this man is going through great distress—to the extent that he puts his face down on a hot stove burner. As he raises his head up, she sees that he seems to be forming something with his hands. Then she sees that he has fashioned a mask of ivory.

The group walked through the steps of the Theme Matrix to see if we could determine what core theme this woman was dreaming. We decided it dealt with theme #1: "What is your personal self-image?" At the moment we said those words, she had what Jeremy Taylor calls an "aha" moment. That is, she came to an awakening of some subconscious truth hiding deep within her. She related that she has recently been working with self-image issues. She has been repeating a self-image release prayer daily. She did not connect this waking-life activity with her dream until it was shown to her by means of the Theme Matrix.

––––––

So far in this book, we have examined themes and how they can be determined and worked with in any context. We have also established a universal core theme model.

Briefly, the six steps involved in working with the Theme Matrix are as follows:

1. Select a dream that sparks emotion or poses questions for you.

2. Ask yourself what question the basic activity is "asking." Is it a question of differentiation, expression, interaction, or capitalization?

3. Ask yourself about the apparent motivation of the character(s). Is it based on sensitivity, will, or intelligence?

4. Find the suggested core theme on the Theme Matrix.

5. Ask yourself if the suggested core theme is logical or feels "right."

6. Use this information for further study on this dream.

You now have the basics for working with themes so that you can incorporate them into your daily dream work. Themes are a key ingredient in the twelve-step process of daily dream work to follow in chapter 3.

three

Incorporating Themes into Dream Work

> *The inquiry into a*
> *dream is another dream.*
> —HALIFAX

Taking responsibility

People today are seeking quick answers to their pressing issues. There is a tendency to want someone to totally solve our problems. Television has given us the false impression that problems can be solved in an hour or even a half-hour. We desire a pill or a quick-fix solution. But we know consciously that this is impossible. We also know that many problems cannot even be totally resolved. When we try to look ahead to see the end of the tunnel, the problem becomes overwhelming to us. We long for a method that allows us to take the next step and feel some sense of accomplishment.

When we hit a bump in the road, run out of gas, or just simply get lost on the way, we seek answers. We want to know what this means and how to get back on the road again. It seems to be part of our nature not to bother looking for these answers when things are going smoothly. In fact, Swiss psychiatrist and visionary Carl Jung felt that real growth comes when things are *not* going smoothly, when we are forced to seek out answers to our conflicts and confusion.

The most common method today is to seek out some outside source. We read a book. We take a class. We visit a therapist or spiritual counselor, or we talk with a family member or a partner. We seek something or someone that will provide a road map, a source of comfort and direction.

But when we do this, we often give up responsibility for our lives. And we know that even an outside source cannot provide guarantees. Also, such sources are not always available when we need them, and frequently they are not reliable.

Is there someone who could possibly understand your inner conflicts? The source of your confusion? Is there a counselor who has been with you throughout your journey and knows your secret goals? The answer is yes. Your counselor is within you. And this counselor speaks to you in your dreams.

However, even with dream interpretation, people have often turned to someone else for help, be it the tribal shaman or the modern day psychotherapist. The dream group is a phenomenon that began in the 1970s and was made popular by Dr. Montague Ullman, a psychotherapist from New York. Dr. Ullman believed that it was possible for people interested in dreams to share dream interpretation efforts with others in groups so long as safeguards, such as confidentiality and respect for the dreamer's authority over the dream, were honored.[8] Information on how to start and run a dream group is covered later in this chapter.

We may go to an outside source for help, but we always need to acknowledge that we are ultimately responsible for our actions. You may share your dreams with a group of like-minded dreamers, but ultimately you are the only one who can say what your dream really means.

One of the reasons people have so much trouble with dreams is that they appear to be difficult to work with. Dreams normally arrive in a form that does not invite easy interpretation or meaning. This chapter presents a simple, workable system you can use individually, with trained counselors, and in dream groups. Regardless of how you work with the system, the assumption is that you are ultimately responsible for your dreams and your life. The system includes twelve steps that will help you quickly get to the core issue each dream is trying to bring to your consciousness. It also offers waking-life suggestions on how to deal with issues raised in dreams.

Steps in working with dreams and themes

What follows are twelve basic steps in working with dreams. They incorporate the Theme Matrix, a listing of twelve theme categories designed to help you relate the themes of your personal dreams to a common set of themes. The Theme Matrix enables you to seek ways of dealing with your current issues and concerns. The particulars of the Theme Matrix are described in greater detail in chapter 2.

As mentioned on pages 11–12 in the introduction, the twelve steps—or dream work processes—are presented in the context of the four major life cycle sequences found in all aspects of nature, such as spring, summer, fall, and winter. Each step or process builds on the one before it, allowing you to experience a complete "life cycle" in your daily dream work.

Steps 1 through 3 describe "springlike" processes of differentiation; they help you to differentiate your areas of daytime and nighttime focus by noting the key events of the day, by determining the theme of the day, and by recording the dream experiences that follow.

Steps 4 through 6 describe "summerlike" processes of expression; they help you to express your dream experiences by noting emotions and feelings, giving a title to each of your dreams, and determining their themes.

Steps 7 through 9 describe "fall-like" processes of interaction; they help you to interact with your dream themes by identifying the relationships between your dream themes, the Theme Matrix, and your past dreams.

Steps 10 through 12 describe "winterlike" processes of capitalization; they help you to benefit from your dreams in waking life by reminiscing on dream themes, going to outside sources for help, and by seeking your own internal guidance.

Step 1: Record day notes

This first step has the same characteristics as theme #1 of the Theme Matrix (chapter 2). It involves observing our outlook on life and how we present ourselves in the world.

- What did you do during the day? For instance, did you work, play, visit, or relax?

- Was there something new that you did, or something that caught your attention?

- Did a particular concern affect your thinking or actions?

- Did you "have words" with anyone? Or did you *not* speak your mind?

- Did you have strong feelings or emotional experiences? For example, were you happy, sad, grateful, fearful, embarrassed, or angry?

All such events and emotions of the day can affect what you dream at night. So your actual work on your dreams should start well before any dream occurs. This is a primary reason to maintain a dream journal.

The dream journal. The dream journal is a running log of your dream life. Since what happens to you during the day affects your dreams, the journal is most effective when you include notes on your daily events and emotions. The journal can be in any form with which you are comfortable. A loose-leaf binder generally works best; it enables you to keep information from many days in one place, and it can be folded open for easy review and subsequent commentary and analysis. You may choose to devote a single page or two for each day, or you may just continue your notes from where you left off the day before—whatever works best for you. Be sure to make journal entries each day, *whether you had a dream the night before or not.*

Initial journal entries. Begin your journal entry for each day with today's date followed by the heading "Day notes." In the "Day notes" area, make a brief entry that captures or reviews the main experiences of the day. Especially note experiences in which you had strong feelings or felt strong emotion. We will cover additional entries to be made in the journal in the steps to follow.

The best time to record day notes. The best time to reflect on the day and comment on it is just before going to bed. Not only is this logical, since most of the day is behind you, but it may also affect your dream recall. Many people who have had trouble recalling dreams in the morning have found that recording daily reflections just before retiring actually improves their dream recall. By working on your dream journal at night, you are, in effect, programming yourself for a rich dream experience. You are telling your subconscious that you are serious about dream work and want to recall dreams.

The nightly review. Another valuable benefit of this nightly reflection is offered by an English woman, Vera Stanley Alder, who has written seven books on esoteric teachings. In her book *The Finding of the Third Eye*, she recommends a nightly review. Her process involves slowly going backward through the day, looking for events that may have brought you out of balance, as well as events that brought wisdom. She says that if we do this, "in sleep we can travel straight through to the heart of things, without being held back to the coarser realms by any tormented 'earthbound' thoughts. Our sleep will therefore be deeper and more refreshing." She goes on to say, "This exercise also helps to etch experience into the memory, thereby avoiding the need for a recapitulation of the events."[9]

Why include emotions in day notes? The events we experience that are charged with emotion are the ones that are most likely to spur us on to new discovery and a higher level of awareness about ourselves and what we need to grow and develop. By examining your dreams and the themes of your dreams, you will begin to see that there is a closer relationship between waking-life emotions and dream-life emotions than there is between symbols. The characters in your dreams may not necessarily bear any resemblance to people or animals or inanimate objects from your waking life, but you will quickly recognize their emotional relationship. Maintaining a daily record of your waking-life emotional activity will help you make these connections from your dreams.

Focus on what's important. Of course, there are no rules for keeping your journal. There is no one right way. The main point is to keep some record of what is important to you. As you become more accustomed to doing this as part of your daily routine, the job will become easier. It will take less and less time to reflect on your day and identify what's important. If you miss what's important, your dreams might remind you! Sometimes the dream you record the next morning triggers some event from the day or days before. You may see a possible connection between the current dream and a previous event or emotion that you didn't record. If this happens, it is a good idea to go back to your journal and add this event or emotion to your day notes.

Progressive dream journal example. Following each of the twelve steps will be a sample dream journal entry based on that step. It will be progressive, building on the step before it, offering a pattern or template for construction of your dream journal. An example of recording day notes is offered below.

> 5/29/03 (Monday):
>
> <u>Day notes:</u> I spent the whole day at home alone. I used this time to work on the book, converting the chapters into a more workable form. It felt good watching the whole process flow more easily.

Step 2: Record the theme or themes of the day

This second step has similar characteristics to theme #2 of the Theme Matrix (chapter 2). It involves differentiating ourselves with respect to the major issues and concerns surrounding how we use our personal power and energy in the world.

What themes are and how to determine them. In chapter 1, we learned that the theme of any event you experience is that important message, idea, or perception that the event is attempting to bring to your conscious mind. Themes can be developed by asking yourself the following questions: (1) What basic activity is going on? (2) What is the major issue concerning the characters? (3) What is the apparent or presumed motivation of the characters that causes them to act in this way? Is it based on sensitivity? Caring, love, or applied wisdom? Will, determination, or manifestations of power? Or thought, reason, and adaptability?

Themes can be stated as full sentences, in a word or a few words, or as a question. Understanding themes comes easiest when they are personalized, are stated in the present tense, and are not just reiterations of the words or actions in the event.

Determine a theme of the day. Review your day notes and write a theme in your dream journal based on the events and emotions of the day. Remember to write the theme in the present tense.

You may find it easy to state a theme that summarizes the events of the day, such as *I am finally able to complete many long-standing chores* or *I am not able to do things I had planned to do.*

If there were many different kinds of activities going on in the day, you may find there were several themes: *I constantly have to wait for others* and *I am able to be sensitive to the needs of others.*

You may just want to write a theme for the most significant activity of the day, the one that had a particular emotional impact. For instance, *I am blessed with a magnificent gift* or *I have discovered something most unexpected.*

Why determine a theme of the day? Themes help you look at your life from a broader perspective. It is so easy to get caught up in the details and lose sight of our overall goals and direction. Looking at daily themes over a period of days and weeks will help you to see patterns in your life. For instance, if you find that you are constantly repeating the theme *I let things get out of control*, perhaps you will want to examine ways to prevent this from happening. Later in this book, we will present ways you can relate your themes of the day to your dream themes; this may be the most valuable use of the daily theme exercise for you.

Find your blessing, challenge, and service. Dr. Carol Parrish-Harra, founder of Sancta Sophia Seminary and the spiritual community of Sparrow Hawk Village in Oklahoma, has added an element to the daily review process. You may find this helpful in determining the theme of the day. She suggests that every day each of us is presented with a blessing, a challenge, and an opportunity to perform service.[10] We might consider that we are blessed when we receive a gift, when we are honored for our creativity or an achievement, or when someone acknowledges love and affection for us. We may be challenged to reevaluate our goals and objectives or to be better communicators or partners. We may be called on to serve by being led to help or nurture a friend or family member or to respect and protect the environment.

The chart on page 59 is a guide to help you determine where you might have received a blessing, a challenge, and an opportunity to serve each day. It is based on the logic in the Theme Matrix. It is just a guide, but it may direct your thinking to finding ways you are blessed, called, and challenged that you had not realized.

Read down the blessing, challenge, and opportunity-to-serve columns and find a statement in each column that best fits a situation you faced today. For instance, you may have received a blessing in the form of a new car, you may have been challenged in some way in your work, and you may have experienced an opportunity to serve by helping your coworkers meet new challenges at work.

As in this example, the theme suggestions will not necessarily be on the same row. The new car "blessing" is found on row 2, "Needs being satisfied." Reading across to the "Which helped you" column, you can see that this blessing is helping you differentiate your personal resources and needs. You may now be able to create a day theme from this, such as *I am learning to differentiate my personal resources and needs by being blessed with a new possession.*

There may be more than one theme per day. The challenge and opportunity-to-serve statements in this example are both on row 6; they serve to help you express your analytical skills. A second day theme based on these statements may be *I am learning to use my analytical skills to express myself in service to others.*

Progressive dream journal example. Following is an example of a dream journal entry based on these first two steps of the twelve steps used in working with dreams and themes:

> 5/29/03 (Monday):
>
> <u>Day notes:</u> I spent the whole day at home alone. I used this time to work on the book, converting the chapters into a more workable form. It felt good watching the whole process flow more easily.
>
> <u>Theme of the day:</u> I am exploring a new approach.

Step 3: Record the dream

This third step has similar characteristics to theme #3 of the Theme Matrix (chapter 2). Here we are concerned with presenting facts and observing how our subconscious mind is communicating what we need to bring into our conscious thought processes.

Capture what you recall. When you awake from a dream, record as much as you can recall. If you don't have time to make a complete entry in your dream journal at that time, jot down enough notes to

THEME-ING THE DAY

Use this chart to help determine where you might have received a blessing, a challenge, and an opportunity to serve each day.

(1) Read down the blessing, challenge, and opportunity-to-serve columns and find a statement in each column that best fits a situation you faced today.

(2) Read across to the "Which helped you" column to see how this experience is helping you learn and develop.

(3) Use these statements to create a theme or themes for the day.

Today you received:	A blessing concerning:	A challenge concerning:	An opportunity to serve by:	Which helped you:
1.	Being accepted	Not being accepted	Helping others feel accepted	Differentiate your personal self-image
2.	Needs being satisfied	Needs not being satisfied	Helping others become self-reliant	Differentiate your personal resources and needs
3.	Functioning or communicating well	Not functioning/communicating well	Helping others function/express themselves	Differentiate your personal thought processes
4.	Being nurtured	Needing care	Nurturing others	Express your feelings and develop stability
5.	Having space to express will	Having limited opportunity	Helping others express will	Express your will, explore and be creative
6.	Experiencing success	Experiencing failure	Helping others meet challenges	Express your analytical skills
7.	Being loved	Feeling threatened	Creating balance in a partnership	Interact by uniting in balance
8.	Being revived or healed	Feeling victimized	Sharing resources and desires	Interact by sharing resources and desires
9.	Being mobile, able to adapt	Feeling immobilized	Acting with broad perspective	Interact by adapting and broadening perspective
10.	Gaining from experience, improving	Failing to gain from experience, falling behind	Making a contribution for mutual benefit of society	Benefit by using what you have learned from past achievements and pain
11.	Being guided, hopeful	Being misled, fearful	Guiding others through proper use of knowledge and truth	Gain from what you know to be truly essential and of value
12.	Being unrestricted, in control	Being restricted, out of control, overwhelmed	Exemplifying how to be joyful and spontaneous yet in control	Realize what you believe about freedom from artificial boundaries

help you bring back the entire dream later: basic locales, characters, activities. It is best to get the dream written up as soon as you can the next day, while it is still fresh in your mind. It is not necessary to write the full narrative of the dream, detailing every event that happened in story form. Not all dreams occur as stories, with one event following the other in chronological order. For instance, artists frequently dream in images and pictures, often with strong emotional content that can't be easily explained in words. Sometimes all you receive is a fragment of a dream. The goal is to get down enough of the key points of the dream to find the message it is trying to convey.

What we recall is what we need. Remember that when you are writing down your dream in your journal, you are dealing with your *memory* of the dream. You may not be able to recall every detail. And you are picking up the story or imagery from a certain point and taking it to another point. This means that what we recall is exactly what is needed to be brought to our waking consciousness at this time—no more, no less. Even the dreams that can't be recalled serve a purpose in your subconscious. Further, if a message really needs to come to consciousness, you will receive it in a future dream.

Write your dream in the present tense. In chapter 1, we emphasized the importance of writing themes in the present tense. This practice is also recommended when writing your dream narrative. The dream is an experience in itself that happens in the present tense. To write in the present tense, we would say, "I am driving my car through the storm." This best captures the "now" sense of the dream's action and keeps it dynamic. It keeps the dream much more new and alive than writing in the past tense. "I drove my car through the storm" or "I had driven my car through the storm" is written in the past tense; this makes it sound done, stagnant, over. Each time we review the dream when it's written in the present tense, we can more easily relive it. We can reenter it—doing what we did and feeling what we felt. This helps us zero in again and again on the dream's meaning. It is also easier for others to enter our dreams and help us explore them. As they listen to us recall—or read—a dream in its present tense, the dream becomes another distinct experience that is occurring at the moment we are recalling it. It's a new event happening right now. By writing in the present tense, the dream continues to be fresh and new and alive.

There's something else to consider here. If you choose to identify a dream as a past event, you might be doing so because the dream's content or message speaks to something you consciously—or unconsciously—choose not to face up to, something you don't want to make part of your current life. So if you are in the habit of writing in the present tense and you notice yourself slipping into past tense, you might want to take a closer look at the issue being dealt with at that point. Is there something you are avoiding? For example, let us suppose you are relating a dream in which you are talking with a waking-life friend. All along you are speaking or writing in the present tense. But at a certain point you find yourself saying, "I got angry with him." The fact that this last statement is presented in the past tense may indicate some suppressed anger you are not willing to face. Who the anger is actually directed to would be the subject of some self-examination. To this waking-life person? To a flaw within yourself that this person represents? Regardless of the issue, pay attention to your past-tense reflections.

Dreams are timeless . . . and writing them in present tense helps keep them so. There are countless stories of people who are still working on dreams they had many years ago. These dreams are as fresh today as they were when first dreamed. Each time you reenter and analyze a dream, it offers you new information for your life today.

Progressive dream journal example. Following is an example of a dream journal entry based on the first three steps, including a sample dream narrative. Note that the date of your journal entry is still the day when you recorded your day notes. The dream may actually happen during the morning of the following day. You may enter the actual date of the dream, if you wish. For instance, "Dream #1 (5/30/03)." Note: If you recall more than one dream, you may wish to record the second and subsequent dreams on separate pages. Allow at least five or six lines of space below each dream for notes in response to the steps or dream work processes yet to be discussed in this chapter.

5/29/03 (Monday):

Day notes: I spent the whole day at home alone. I used this time to work on the book, converting the chapters into a more workable form. It felt good watching the whole process flow more easily.

Theme of the day: I am exploring a new approach.

Dream #1: I am with others visiting someone's house. It is a large place but not too well arranged or decorated. I go off alone to investigate since I have not been in this house before. I go downstairs to the lowest level. Of major concern to me is a heater sitting in the center of a tiled triangular space in the corner of a room. The floor in front of the heater slants away from it, and these little black pellets, which I assume are coals, roll all over the floor. While the other people are otherwise occupied, I begin to redesign the house. I build a wall to close off this heater section, creating a utility room. I then create a bathroom near that room. I create a really nice house entry to the left of the bathroom, with steps coming down from above.

Step 4: Determine emotions and feelings

This fourth step has the same characteristics as theme #4 of the Theme Matrix (chapter 2). Here you are concerned with feelings you express or the expected feelings you fail to express in your dreams.

Stick to the dream. You begin to actually work with the dream at this point. It's important to remember that you are just working with the dream itself. You are not trying to incorporate anything from your waking life. Waking-life experiences and events will often appear in your dreams. But this does not mean that your dreams are just repeat performances of daily life. Dreams always offer deeper insight. If you start to relate things that happen in the dream to your waking life too soon, you might begin to analyze the dream. You might come to rapid conclusions as to its meaning, which can cause you to decide to ignore the dream altogether.

For example, assume you have had the following dream:

> I am serving cocoa and going around singing to every-one on one floor of our office. I have a large pail of cocoa I have prepared. I go to the next floor up, plan-ning to do the same with them. I have about a half a pail of cocoa. As I come up to that floor, I look down the hall. A woman comes out of her office and calls to me that they need the cocoa and singing up here. But I go around to offices and do not feel they are into it. I can't seem to motivate myself to begin.

Suppose, on the day before having this dream, you had been in-volved in an office party in which you were joining others going through the office singing and serving cocoa. Your tendency would be to write this dream off as just a replay of the day's experience. You might miss the subtle reference at the end of the dream to a lack of motivation, possibly indicating some insecurity in dealing with others. Rather than ignoring the dream, you perhaps should ask yourself some questions regarding incidents in the dream that were not the same as in the waking-life experience, such as why this worked on one floor but not the next, or why you are not so motivated when trying to do this alone. Dreams always offer deeper insight than what is on the surface.

Why consider emotions from your dreams? In step 1, you were advised to record the emotions of your waking life because of the close relationship between waking-life emotions and dream-life emotions. Using the cocoa dream example from above, you may not have had any experience in waking life involving singing in the office or doling out cocoa. But the emotions associated with "lack of motivation" or feelings of insecurity reflected in the dream may directly relate to behaviors you are dealing with or need to deal with. As we noted in step 1, the characters in your dreams may not necessarily bear any resemblance to people or animals or inanimate objects from your waking life. Consequently, the activities in your dreams may not bear any resemblance to waking-life activities, but their emotional relationship usually "hits home."

Record emotions or feelings. Emotions and feelings fall into three categories: emotions you or the other characters displayed in the dream, emotions or feelings you would expect to be expressed but are not expressed by you or the other characters in the dream, and your emotions on waking. Record any or all of these that you encounter. Emotions are not always easy to find in the dream. But do attempt to write two or three feeling words based on what you are experiencing in the dream or on what other characters in the dream are experiencing. Whether you can name the feelings in your dreams or not, you should be able to capture the feelings you had from the dream experience upon awakening. Consider the following dream experience:

> I am on a cement deck, like a pavilion that goes out into the ocean. I observe a woman who has a strange way of dancing. She leans back and extends her arms to the sides, rocking back and forth, side to side. People begin dancing, so I go out and try to dance like she does, even though I feel it is silly. Then I look out to the ocean and see an enormous wave coming. I warn the others. We don't have time to run inside before it hits the deck. No one is hurt, but the deck is flooded and we need to stop. I see more and more high waves coming. It must be a major storm. I go inside. A woman has been collecting money for this dance and says we took in over $1,000.

Here, the dreamer seems to be expressing some anxiety about the waves coming in and nervousness about the possible danger to the dancers. On waking, he or she might feel this anxiety or not. It is interesting to note in this dream that the woman at the end is more interested in the money taken in than the ensuing storm. If this were your dream, what would that mean to you?

Emotions as the theme. There is another reason why recording the emotional aspect of dreams is important. Expressed—or unexpressed—emotions are helpful in determining the theme. In fact, they might be the theme! Idly watching brutality might indicate a theme in your life of not being able to take action when called upon. This may be a personal characteristic. Inaction in the face of a lion might indicate a theme of avoidance of responsibility. Following is an example of a dream in which writing comments on emotions helped determine the theme:

> I am staying at a place, or visiting. I am naked and go
> into a room. A woman is vacuuming in the next room,
> so I close the door. But there is a wide gap in the door
> frame, so I figure she can see me anyhow. I need to
> use the bathroom. But I find that my old high school
> buddy is in there taking a shower, so I have to wait. Fi-
> nally he comes out and I go in. I walk to the sink area
> and am surprised to find the shower still on. I actually
> walk right under it and get my head wet. I go ahead and
> shower but then wonder if I'm supposed to just leave
> the shower running when I'm done, as he did.

The dreamer felt strong concern about being seen naked and doing the right thing. The theme he came up with was *I am concerned about doing the proper thing*. This may be characteristic behavior for the dreamer.

Progressive dream journal example. Following is an example of a dream journal entry based on the first four steps, including emotion/feeling comments relating to the sample dream narrative.

5/29/03 (Monday):

<u>Day notes:</u> I spent the whole day at home alone. I used this time to work on the book, converting the chapters into a more workable form. It felt good watching the whole process flow more easily.

<u>Theme of the day:</u> I am exploring a new approach.

<u>Dream #1:</u> I am with others visiting someone's house. It is a large place but not too well arranged or decorated. I

go off alone to investigate since I have not been in this house before. I go downstairs to the lowest level. Of major concern to me is a heater sitting in the center of a tiled triangular space in the corner of a room. The floor in front of the heater slants away from it, and these little black pellets, which I assume are coals, roll all over the floor. While the other people are otherwise occupied, I begin to redesign the house. I build a wall to close off this heater section, creating a utility room. I then create a bathroom near that room. I create a really nice house entry to the left of the bathroom, with steps coming down from above.

<u>Emotions:</u> Feel the need to be alone, away from others. Not concerned that this is not my house that I am changing. Pleased with what I have done.

Step 5: Determine a title

This fifth step has the same characteristics as theme #5 of the Theme Matrix (chapter 2). Here you are expressing your creativity to clearly identify the dream. Your goal is to eliminate confusion and uncertainty. And this is exactly what a dream title does for a dream . . . and a dreamer.

Why give a dream a title? The simplest and easiest thing you can do to begin understanding a dream is to give it a title. The title directs your energy to the most significant aspect or aspects of the dream. The process of writing a title helps you determine what is most important in the dream to you, the dreamer.

A woman was sharing her dream in a dream group. At the very end, a kangaroo appeared, just for a second. She told the group that she had given this dream the title "The kangaroo." This title seemed to be far removed from what others in the group expected. Most would have probably dealt more with the action up to that point. But the kangaroo is what had the most impact on that woman at that time. So "The kangaroo" may have been the best title for her, as it expressed what was most important *to her*.

It is important to identify what is most important to you in the title because that is most likely what will trigger memory of the entire dream for you.

What does a title have to do with themes? Later in this process of working with dreams and dream themes—when you are looking at your dreams that have the same or similar themes—you'll want to look at the title. If you have written the title well, you will be able to tell the context in which the dream's theme is being expressed.

For instance, the woman in the example above who titled her dream simply "The kangaroo" can expect to have trouble differentiating it from other kangaroo dreams she may have over time. The kangaroo isn't in any kind of context. If you have a kangaroo dream, you *will* be able to tell this one from another if you describe in the title what is unique about this particular kangaroo. For example, "The kangaroo that chases me into the elevator," as differentiated from "The kangaroo that sits with me at the office."

What's in a title? A good way to get used to designing titles is to pick up your daily newspaper and see how the writers and editors title their news stories. If news headlines are written well, you should be able to scan the page and have a pretty good idea what the main news stories are about. They should answer the who, what, when, and where questions. Who was involved in the news story? What were they doing? When did it happen? Where did the action take place? Sometimes the "why" of the activity is also apparent in a headline, although motive or intent is not always known as a news story is first investigated.

Consider the headline "Strong earthquake hits northeast Japan." Here we know who was most affected (the Japanese), what took place (an earthquake), and generally where it happened (a specific area of Japan). If the article appeared in today's paper, we can assume the "when" was sometime in the past twenty-four hours. We can assume it was a rather significant earthquake if it warranted being included in the newspaper. The question of why this happened is perhaps covered in the article; for instance, it may have been caused by a particular shift in certain tectonic plates under or near Japan.

Consider the following dream:

> I hurl some sort of red rectangular thing at an inset in a wall. It sticks perfectly in the center. For some reason, I feel I need to keep trying to do this, perhaps to improve, even though the first one was perfectly centered. But each time I try to do this again, I end up throwing four red dots of paint way off center, hitting the side walls. I can't seem to get it right anymore.

A possible title for this dream is "I keep throwing red dots at wall, after perfect throw the first time." From this title we know who was involved in the action ("I," the dreamer), what happened (throwing red dots), and where it happened (at a wall). We have some concept of "when," in that there is a distinct passage of time from "the first time" to subsequent throws. You could include "for some reason" in the title to address the purpose or intent of the action, although the real intent does not seem to be known.

There are often cases in dreams where you encounter two or more distinct activities going on in different locales with different characters. In this case, you may need to add a subtitle to your dream. For instance, the following dream has two distinct types of activity happening in two different locales.

> I am trying to reach someone for help. I use my mobile phone, but I just get a long commercial pitch from a woman. It is probably just a recording, but nothing I would expect on my phone. I go upstairs in the house I am visiting. I am staying in something like a loft above a bedroom. I climb up there and see a cat coming toward me across the bed. Then a smaller cat comes out from under the covers. It has beautiful bluish-silver fur and blue eyes. I have never seen a blue cat before. It comes right to me and cuddles.

A suggested title for this dream is "I get commercial message on mobile phone, then find blue cat in my bed." You may choose to state them as separate sentences or separate the two thoughts by a semicolon. In any case, both titles include some information on the who, what, and where issues in the dream.

Think of your dream titles as headlines. Include enough of the who, what, and where—perhaps when and why—information that will help you recall your entire dream long after the dream occurred—perhaps years later.

Progressive dream journal example. Following is an example of a dream journal entry based on the first five steps, including determination of a title for the dream:

5/29/03 (Monday):

Day notes: I spent the whole day at home alone. I used this time to work on the book, converting the chapters into a more workable form. It felt good watching the whole process flow more easily.

<u>Theme of the day:</u> I am exploring a new approach.

<u>Dream #1:</u> I am with others visiting someone's house. It is a large place but not too well arranged or decorated. I go off alone to investigate since I have not been in this house before. I go downstairs to the lowest level. Of major concern to me is a heater sitting in the center of a tiled triangular space in the corner of a room. The floor in front of the heater slants away from it, and these little black pellets, which I assume are coals, roll all over the floor. While the other people are otherwise occupied, I begin to redesign the house. I build a wall to close off this heater section, creating a utility room. I then create a bathroom near that room. I create a really nice house entry to the left of the bathroom, with steps coming down from above.

<u>Emotions:</u> Feel the need to be alone, away from others. Not concerned that this is not my house that I am changing. Pleased with what I have done.

<u>Title:</u> I redesign the lowest level of a house, enclosing a heater in triangular space.

Step 6: Determine a theme

This sixth step has the same characteristics as theme #6 of the Theme Matrix (chapter 2). Here you are using your innate analytical ability to express the key message or messages of the dream.

What themes are and how to determine them. In chapter 1, we learned that the theme of any event you experience is that important message, idea, or perception that the event is attempting to bring to your conscious mind. Themes can be developed by asking yourself the following questions:

(1) What basic activity is going on?

(2) What is the major issue concerning the characters?

(3) What is the apparent or presumed motivation of the characters that causes them to act in this way? Is it based on sensitivity, caring, love, or applied wisdom? Will, determination, or manifestations of power? Or thought, reason, and adaptability?

Themes can be stated as full sentences, in a word or a few words, or as a question. Understanding themes comes easiest when they are personalized, are stated in the present tense, and are not just reiterations of the words or actions in the event.

Why bother with the theme? Isn't it enough to determine the title? Determining the title for your dream may help you see what in the dream is most significant, in terms of characters and activity. But working on the theme requires that you deal with the real issue the dream is trying to present. Titles are more likely to deal with symbols. Themes deal with life issues. Titles deal with surface material. Themes explore the dream's meaning. Titles help you understand what is going on *in the dreams*. Themes help you deal with what is going on *in your life*. This will become clearer as we pursue the steps to follow. For instance, in step 8, you will learn how you can relate your dream themes to the themes of the day; this may be the most valuable use of dream themes for you.

Determine a theme for your dream. Using the guidelines in chapter 1, as summarized above, review your dream and write its theme in your dream journal.

Your theme may actually summarize the entire dream. For instance, in step 5 above, we examined a dream entitled "I keep throwing red dots at wall, after perfect throw the first time." A generalized theme dealing with the major issue in this dream would be *I am attempting to improve on perfection.*

The other example in step 5 was a dream that consisted of two separate activities involving different characters. In this case, you may look for a theme that incorporates both activities. This dream example was entitled "I get commercial message on mobile phone, then find blue cat in my bed." Here is a suggested theme for this dream that covers both aspects: *Machine doesn't work as it should, but I find something good I've never seen before.* You may wish to state these as two separate themes or separate them by a semicolon.

Progressive dream journal example. Following is an example of a dream journal entry based on the first six steps, including determination of a theme for the dream:

> 5/29/03 (Monday):
>
> <u>Day notes:</u> I spent the whole day at home alone. I used this time to work on the book, converting the chapters into a more workable form. It felt good watching the whole process flow more easily.
>
> <u>Theme of the day:</u> I am exploring a new approach.
>
> <u>Dream #1:</u> I am with others visiting someone's house. It is a large place but not too well arranged or decorated. I go off alone to investigate since I have not been in this house before. I go downstairs to the lowest level. Of major concern to me is a heater sitting in the center of a tiled triangular space in the corner of a room. The floor in front of the heater slants away from it, and these little black pellets, which I assume are coals, roll all over the floor. While the other people are otherwise occupied, I begin to redesign the house. I build a wall to close off

this heater section, creating a utility room. I then create a bathroom near that room. I create a really nice house entry to the left of the bathroom, with steps coming down from above.

Emotions: Feel the need to be alone, away from others. Not concerned that this is not my house that I am changing. Pleased with what I have done.

Title: I redesign the lowest level of a house, enclosing a heater in triangular space.

Theme: Improving newfound space that I do not own.

Step 7: Interact with the dream theme by relating it to the Theme Matrix

This seventh step has the same characteristics as theme #7 of the Theme Matrix (chapter 2). Here you work on developing a "partnership" with your theme and the core themes in the Theme Matrix. You do this by exploring the Theme Matrix to find those core themes that best relate to the theme of your dream.

The Theme Matrix was explained in greater detail in chapter 2. This step involves using the matrix to further understand the question your subconscious mind is asking you to investigate. This question is an issue or concern you are dealing with—or being asked to deal with—in your life.

How to find your core theme in the Theme Matrix. The steps you can use to find your core theme are described in chapter 2. They are summarized briefly here.

First, ask yourself what question the basic activity is asking. One of the following four general questions or activities will apply. These are based on the concept that all life activity can be described in terms of the four life cycles or processes: differentiation, expression, interaction, and capitalization.

- How do you differentiate yourself from others?
- How do you develop self-expression for interaction with others?
- How do you interact with others?
- How are you benefiting from your experiences and realizations?

Second, determine the apparent or presumed motivation of the character or characters. One of the following three general questions will apply. These are based on the concept that all motivation can be described in terms of three types of energy: sensitivity, will, and intelligence.

- Is the activity motivated by sensitivity, caring, love, or applied wisdom?
- Is the activity motivated by will, determination, or manifestations of power?
- Is the activity motivated by thought, reason, or adaptability?

Third, using the Theme Matrix chart on pages 44–45, look down the activity column and across the motivation row to find the suggested core theme or issue for your dream. For example, assume you have a dream that you are naked in public and feel awkward or embarrassed. You, the main dream character, feel separate and apart from the other characters. You are not dressed as they are. You are not like them at this moment. This is an activity involving differentiation. You are not expressing, or interacting, or gaining from what you have learned from this. You are differentiating yourself from others. Your motivation is one of sensitivity. You are in a feeling, sensory mode, not yet expressing your will or power or using reasoning to get yourself out of this situation. The core theme or issue then would be #1: What is your personal self-image? Who are you?

Fourth, examine the core question and the suggested activities listed with the core theme you have found. Does this fit logically with your dream? Does it feel right to you? For instance, in chapter 2 we examined the three different ways you, the dreamer, may behave in the "naked in public" dream. You may be embarrassed (core theme #1), self-reliant (core theme #2), or decisive (core theme #3).

In your dream journal, record the number of the theme and any remarks that led you to think this model theme is where your individual dream theme applies. This will help you recall your logic when you refer to this dream at a later date.

Examples. Here are some examples of theme relationships based on dream activity.

> I need to go over some papers or plans in private, so I take them to a bathroom. I sit on the toilet, then realize there is a large picture window just across from me. I already have my pants down, but I get up to see if I can close the blinds or something. The window seems to change shape as I work with it. Finally I find blinds I can pull down. I think there may be another picture window across from this one, to the left of the toilet.

The title given to this dream is "Having to close blinds on picture window across from toilet." The theme: *Trying to ensure my privacy*. This theme relates to core theme #1 on the Theme Matrix; it definitely relates to the safety, innocence, and self-protection activities involved in the core theme concerning personal self-image.

Here is another dream:

> I am looking at the new Target store being built. I
> build up a mechanical rig that I can use to go across
> the beams and retrieve things from below. I have the rig
> go across the beams rather than in the same direction as
> the beams. I use it repeatedly.

The title for this dream: "I build mechanical rig across beams at new Target store." And the theme: *I create something that helps me function.* This too is related to how the dreamer differentiates himself, but it has more to do with reasoning and strategizing. This relates more to core theme #3, involving synthesizing personal thought to function better.

Progressive dream journal example. Following is an example of a dream journal entry based on the first seven steps, including relating the dream theme to the Theme Matrix:

> 5/29/03 (Monday):
>
> <u>Day notes:</u> I spent the whole day at home alone. I used this time to work on the book, converting the chapters into a more workable form. It felt good watching the whole process flow more easily.
>
> <u>Theme of the day:</u> I am exploring a new approach.
>
> <u>Dream #1:</u> I am with others visiting someone's house. It is a large place but not too well arranged or decorated. I go off alone to investigate since I have not been in this house before. I go downstairs to the lowest level. Of major concern to me is a heater sitting in the center of a tiled triangular space in the corner of a room. The floor in front of the heater slants away from it, and

these little black pellets, which I assume are coals, roll all over the floor. While the other people are otherwise occupied, I begin to redesign the house. I build a wall to close off this heater section, creating a utility room. I then create a bathroom near that room. I create a really nice house entry to the left of the bathroom, with steps coming down from above.

Emotions: Feel the need to be alone, away from others. Not concerned that this is not my house that I am changing. Pleased with what I have done.

Title: I redesign the lowest level of a house, enclosing a heater in triangular space.

Theme: Improving newfound space that I do not own.

Theme Matrix: Relates to core theme #5, discovering new expressions of creativity.

Step 8: Interact with the theme by relating it to the theme(s) of the day

This eighth step has the same characteristics as theme #8 of the Theme Matrix (chapter 2). Here you are seeking to incorporate input from the unconscious—from your dreams—with daily consciousness.

Where in your life . . . ? When people know others who are actively involved in working with dreams, they like to ask them about a recent dream they had—"What does my dream mean?" A common response to this will be, "Where in your life are you acting like the character in your dream?" or, "Where in your life are you going through something similar to what is happening in this dream?" This quick analysis method is used frequently by dream workers. This "where in your life" approach is crucial to the process of understanding your dreams.

We noted earlier that waking-life events rarely, if ever, repeat exactly in dreams. However, the themes of daily life do appear in dreams. From this standpoint, dream life mirrors waking life. This axiom might be restated as: "Dream themes mirror waking themes." So it is important to ask yourself how you can relate your dreams to your waking life. Ask yourself, "Where in my life am I acting out this theme?" and, "Where in my life is this theme being presented to me?" Do the theme or themes of the day in waking life—those you identified in step 2 of this process—relate to the theme of last night's dream? How about the themes of the past few days?

Before examining an example of this step, let's look at another suggestion that you might want to incorporate into your daily dream work routine: relating the day theme to the matrix.

Relate your theme of the day to the Theme Matrix. Another step that will help you see the relationship between day themes and dream themes involves relating the themes of the day to the core themes in the Theme Matrix. At this point, or as you are writing your theme of the day, use the procedure in step 7 to look at the Theme Matrix chart and determine to which core theme your theme of the day relates. For instance, if your theme of the day is *I am finally able to complete many long-standing chores*, the core theme most closely relates to core theme #6, meeting challenges through the expression of personal skill. The theme of the day *I constantly have to wait for others* has to do with powerlessness and self-reliance, core theme #2. Record what you feel are the core theme relationships in your dream journal.

The dream experience in the progressive dream journal example is a rather convenient example of this. The theme of the day is *I am exploring a new approach*. This theme relates to core theme #5 in the Theme Matrix. This is indicated by the fact that the day dealt with personal exploration and creativity. The theme of the dream that night is *Improving newfound space that I do not own*. This theme also relates to model theme #5, as it deals with discovering new expressions of creativity. This example, of course, would come as no surprise to one involved in a creative process, such as writing almost daily.

However, you may note that the theme of this dream brings up an issue that perhaps was not noticed in evaluating the theme of the day or even the details of the dream itself. The dream is telling the dreamer that there is some personal creative work that he or she does "not own." If this were your dream, you might want to question in what aspect of your waking-life creativity you are not willing to accept responsibility. Is there some creative work you are afraid to tackle for some reason? Are you procrastinating? Are you relying on someone else to take over? On the other hand, are you attempting to help someone who perhaps does not want your help? Are you getting involved in something that is none of your business? What does "do not own" mean to you?

Dreams raise issues that may not be in waking consciousness and may be demanding attention. Sometimes the messages are very subtle, as we saw in this last example. Comparing the theme of the day to the theme of your dream is an excellent tool you can use to bring these issues to light.

Step 8, relating the theme of the day to the dream theme or themes, will help you to identify what is of chief importance in your life right now. It is likely that your most recent dream will not exactly relate to the theme of the most recent day or the past few days. Dreams do not always come in such convenient order. If this is true, don't despair. Simply skip this step for now, as the next step is designed to deal with just this situation. It helps you examine trends in your dream themes.

Progressive dream journal example.

5/29/03 (Monday):

Day notes: I spent the whole day at home alone. I used this time to work on the book, converting the chapters into a more workable form. It felt good watching the whole process flow more easily.

Theme of the day: I am exploring a new approach.

Theme Matrix: Relates to theme #5, personal exploration, creativity.

Dream #1: I am with others visiting someone's house. It is a large place but not too well arranged or decorated. I go off alone to investigate since I have not been in this house before. I go downstairs to the lowest level. Of major concern to me is a heater sitting in the center of a tiled triangular space in the corner of a room. The floor in front of the heater slants away from it, and these little black pellets, which I assume are coals, roll all over the floor. While the other people are otherwise occupied, I begin to redesign the house. I build a wall to close off this heater section, creating a utility room. I then create a bathroom near that room. I create a really nice house entry to the left of the bathroom, with steps coming down from above.

Emotions: Feel the need to be alone, away from others. Not concerned that this is not my house that I am changing. Pleased with what I have done.

Title: I redesign the lowest level of a house, enclosing a heater in triangular space.

Theme: Improving newfound space that I do not own.

Theme Matrix: Relates to theme #5, discovering new expressions of creativity. (Note that the theme of the day also relates to theme #5; entry can be made here or above, as shown.)

Step 9: Interact with the theme of the dream by relating it to other dreams

This ninth step has the same characteristics as theme #9 of the Theme Matrix (chapter 2). Here you are following a logical process to explore your dreams from a broader perspective.

Recurring themes. The first way to work with the issues of your dreams is to look for how the themes of dreams repeat themselves. You may find that you have a dream over and over again, at various times, with essentially the same characters, symbols, and activities, with minor modifications. This is called a recurring dream. Assume you are repeatedly having a dream in which you find yourself naked in a crowded school hallway. Being naked in public is a common dream experienced throughout the world. We noted in step 7, when working with the Theme Matrix, that the "naked in public" dreams may not all necessarily be presenting the same message or theme. For instance, if the dream character is taking on more of an active role and is using logic to correct this situation, theme #1—personal self-image—is not as much the issue as is theme #6, which concerns using analytical ability to meet a challenge.

On the other hand, you may find that you have a series of dreams—again, not necessarily sequential—all with the same theme. The characters, symbols, and activities may be entirely different. But by identifying the theme of each dream and seeing its relationship within the Theme Matrix, you will see that you are experiencing recurring themes. A message is attempting to come to consciousness using many different scenarios. It is seeking a form that you will understand and act upon. For example, consider the following two dreams:

> Dream #1: It is late at night. I am to get a valuable form of some sort. I want it, but the man who is giving it to me feels he needs to explain it all in great detail. I get annoyed and wish he would get it over with. No one else is around. I'm afraid if he doesn't give it to me soon, someone will come and mess it up for me, like they will say I'm not the one to get it. I actually feel the form is more important to the other man than it is to me. I don't care about the details like he does. I just want to get it.

> Dream #2: I am leaving with several others in a van. I think I am the driver, and it is a man and a woman I am taking. I think I am driving them to work. But there is much confusion and they do not cooperate with me and delay our departure.

These two dreams have entirely different characters and settings. The action is quite different in each dream. But both dreams share certain commonalities. In both dreams there is something the dreamer wants and is delayed in getting by others: the valuable form in the first dream, the urgency to drive the others to work in the second. In each, the dreamer is unable to express personal will, consistent with core theme #5 in the Theme Matrix. These two dreams are sending a message that if the dreamer wants to receive what is wanted in a timely fashion, he or she needs to express it to others, especially when they are the ones responsible for delaying progress.

Recurring dreams and dreams in series with recurring themes are both attempting to bring messages to your consciousness. In both cases, you are being presented with issues that in some way need further attention.

Well-written dream titles that include information on the main characters and symbols help you see the relationships between recurring dreams. Well-stated dream themes help you see the relationship between dreams with similar themes. The following suggestion will be of assistance in both cases.

Maintain a list of your dream titles and themes. In his workshops, Jeremy Taylor recommends that you maintain a list of your dreams by date and title. But you can expand on that idea. Including your dream themes and their relation to the Theme Matrix on this chronological listing will help you to see at a glance what themes are recurring in your dream life. Following are some title/theme entries:

Date	Title	Theme	Relation to Matrix
5/3/03	Family avoids dinner; kids knock down wall	Annoyance at incompletion and lack of concern by others	#5: desires not being satisfied
5/4/03	I observe things pushing through underground tunnels	Ability to meet and overcome obstacles	#5: goals met through will and determination
5/5/03	Frozen water found on bookcases at our enormous estate	Find something disturbing when exploring new spaces	#5: exploring, but finding something unsatisfying, perhaps threatening
5/6/03	I give little dented car to man	Finding joy in imperfect, simple thing	#12: experiencing inner joy without limitations
5/7/03	Two alligators slide out of bag for my wife	Enjoying something that should be frightening	#12: choosing joy over fear of shadowy stuff
5/8/03	My yellow Cadillac goes down ramp and three men threaten to take it	I let my possessions get away from me	#2: concern for material loss

These few examples provide some interesting material for observation. If you just look down the list of titles, you would assume these dreams bear no relation to each other. But the themes reflect definite relationships between dreams, especially when identified by the core themes in the matrix.

For example, the themes in the first three dreams appear to be somewhat different but can each be related to core theme #5, dealing with personal will being met or not being met. Even though the themes and core theme relationships are different in the six dreams listed, there seems to be a general running theme of the dreamer's concern for having needs met, whether in terms of resources or expected services. Resources and services are both being given and received. There is joy found in giving and receiving when personal will can be actively expressed. There is apparent anxiety found when the loss of possessions or the ability to express personal will is threatened. Such observations should excite the dreamer to further investigation. The most lucrative area to examine is waking life.

Steps 10 through 12 to follow offer suggestions on ways to delve more deeply into this issue of the relationship between the themes presented in your dreams and where in your life you are experiencing these themes.

Progressive dream journal example. The theme of our progressive example is *Improving newfound space that I do not own*. This relates to core theme #5 in the Theme Matrix, in that it involves discovering new expressions of creativity. Since our example does not include other dreams with which to relate this one, let's assume this is the same dreamer as the one who had the six dreams just discussed above. Using available space in the journal, the dreamer may make an entry such as the following:

Relation to other dreams: Note dreams of 5/3, 5/4, 5/5, all relating to core theme #5, especially 5/5, in which I am exploring but finding something unsatisfying.

Step 10: Benefit from the dream by reminiscing on dream themes

This tenth step has the same characteristics as theme #10 of the Theme Matrix (chapter 2). Here you are gaining from the wisdom presented in your dreams. You see how the dreams are bringing issues to your consciousness relating to waking-life achievements and painful experiences so that you can seek renewal, healing, and transformation.

Note: In the chapter to follow, the matrix offers suggestions on specific actions you can take in your waking life to benefit from the message the dream is presenting. This is called "honoring" your dream. Honoring opens you up to the next question. Steps 10 through 12 also describe ways of benefiting from or capitalizing on the messages in your dream, but honoring is of such importance that the entire chapter 4 to follow will be devoted to it.

Again, where in your life . . . ? In step 8, you were presented with the concept of looking for the relationship between the theme of the day and the themes of dreams you had following that day. You were encouraged to ask yourself the question, "Where in my life is this theme occurring?" By doing this, you begin to see how the themes of your dreams relate to the themes of your waking life. Dreams point out issues or questions or concerns you need to work with in your waking life.

In step 9, you were encouraged to look for recurring themes over a longer period of time. By doing this, you can begin to realize that your dreams may not deal with waking-life themes of the previous day or even the past few days. More likely, they will deal with trends in your life and issues you may not yet have recognized as significant.

For example, you may begin having dreams with the recurring theme of your concern about the feelings of another. You examine the themes of the past few days and see nothing that would indicate a relationship between this theme and what is going on in current waking life. You look back through your title/theme list and see that you have had dreams with this theme at various times in the past. You look at the dates and see that those dreams came around the time you were visiting a close relative who was quite ill. You ask yourself, "Why is this theme repeating itself now?" You realize that in your involvement with current work pressures, you have forgotten that you are still concerned about that relative. Your subconscious mind is attempting to remind you that you still need to express your feelings for this person. The individual in question may never appear in your dreams, even symbolically. But the recurring theme is bringing this issue back to your consciousness.

Steps 8 and 9 help you determine the relationships between your dream themes and the themes of your life. Step 10 is the first of three steps designed to help you gain from what you have learned and apply it to your waking life. It is one thing to identify an issue, question, or concern, and quite another thing to face it and deal with it. But this step is necessary for beginning your healing, transformation, and self-renewal.

This step shows you how to use the magic of the dreams themselves to help you capitalize on the issues they present. It does not involve expressing your will or determination to understand theme relationships, as in step 8. It does not involve use of the logical mind, as in step 9. What you are seeking to do here is tap the magic of your inner wisdom. This wisdom has developed over the years based on your experiences—positive and negative.

Start by lessening conscious control. Veronica Tonay is a clinical psychologist practicing in Santa Cruz, California. In her book *The Art of Dreaming*, she addresses the similarity between the dream process and the waking-life creative process:

> "When creative people create by allowing their minds
> to relax, lessening conscious control over their thoughts,
> original images burst forth. This process then reverses itself, and consciousness resumes control, synthesizing
> whatever has appeared to produce our creative work.
> This is exactly what happens when we go to sleep and
> dream, then awaken and consciously recall our
> dreams."[11]

Tonay offers several ways to revisit your dreams, viewing them as vehicles to inspire your own innate creativity. All involve lessening conscious control over your thoughts. She recommends choosing an activity that you would not normally do. For instance, if you are a writer, choose to dance or paint.

- Draw or paint the images in the dream exactly as they occurred or as you would recreate them.

- Write stories that have nothing to do with your dream, using key words or phrases in the dream that evoke emotion. Or write a poem using these phrases.

- Put dream feelings and interactions into motion; dance the dream.

- Create a photomontage of your dream, using images from your local environment.

- Act out the story of your dream as if it were a play.[12]

Activities carried out in this space of reduced conscious control not only awaken your creativity, they help trigger old memories. They heighten your ability to recall suppressed thoughts and issues. As you are engaged in some artistic endeavor regarding your dream, allow yourself to think about the past. Accept whatever comes to mind as a synchronistic message. It might be a flash of memory about a recent or distant event in your life. A person. A movie. Some school experience. At this point, reverse the process. Stop and reflect on this. What did you learn from that event? That person? Are you still carrying around some old "stuff" that you thought you had let go of long ago? Is the dream offering new insight? How does this memory relate to anything you are going through at the present time?

This method is especially well suited for recurring dreams.

Recurring themes. An excellent method of seeking out and examining recurring themes is offered by Jungian analyst and veteran dream worker Robert Bosnak. This method also involves lessening conscious control.

In his masterful book *Tracks in the Wilderness of Dreaming*, Bosnak provides a method for mapping a dream series—a set of concurrent dreams. The process involves seeking out similar images in these dreams and placing them in "clusters" for further creative work. These clusters are, in effect, life themes. Bosnak believes they provide "tracks" that help us wander through the "wilderness" of the dream world.[13]

Bosnak recommends you work with fewer than twenty dreams. You don't want to overwhelm yourself with this. However, the examples he offers in the book are from fifty-three consecutive dreams taken from seven weeks of his dream log.

Bosnak has you print out your dreams on separate sheets of paper and tape them together, creating an accordion foldout. Then you connect similar images, such as "long tables," and identify clusters or themes. Bosnak noted that his "long table" images related to themes of marriage, depression, and loneliness in the dreams. These connected themes became his first cluster.

The next two steps in his process involve what he calls "musing" and "reminiscence." Here you muse upon and write down whatever comes to mind from the themes, and then reminisce about the past. These are the ways you begin to integrate the dream themes into your waking-life consciousness.

The process does not stop there. It is only the beginning. Bosnak then asks you to write a descriptive paragraph about each element—each dream statement—in the cluster, in chronological order. Then he has you use various formats or genres to rewrite what you have done in step 6. Examples he gives of this are letters to himself and others, travelogues, poems, and statements of commentary to himself.

Note also that Bosnak is not just working with the symbols alone. He might find a recurring symbol, such as long tables, but he investigates the activity that is going on concerning these symbols. He recognizes that a recurrent theme emerges involving long tables, which he can then examine.

Progressive dream journal example. As an example of Bosnak's method, let's examine the six dreams from the title/theme list in step 9. To complete the exercise properly, we need to view each dream in its entirety. For the sake of space, some of the dreams are summarized. Assume the following dreams have been recorded on single pages, taped together in chronological order.

(1) 5/3/03: <u>Title:</u> Family avoids dinner; kids knock down wall.

I am in a house. I seem to be waiting for dinner. I get annoyed when my family just goes outside rather than dealing with dinner. I watch as kids climb on what looks like a well-built stone wall, to find them knocking down the stones along the top.

(2) 5/4/03: <u>Title:</u> I observe things pushing through underground tunnels.

I see things pushing large openings or horizontal tunnels underground. I am especially interested in a white thing that appears to be soft and quite flexible. It is able to maneuver through almost anything.

(3) 5/5/03: <u>Title:</u> Frozen water found on bookcases at our enormous estate.

I am with my wife in our enormous house. It almost feels like we have this one in addition to our smaller house. I need something from the back room. I actually had forgotten we had it. It is a long room that runs the width of the back of the house. I look at the bookcases that are on both sides of the entryway back to the main house. They go all the way to the high ceiling. On the right side, up near the top, I see where water has come out of an opening and frozen. I go to the left bookcase and see the same thing has happened there. I go back to my wife and try to tell her about this, but my words get all confused. I begin to look for the tall ladder, so I can investigate the problem and perhaps fix it.

(4) 5/6/03: <u>Title:</u> I give little dented car to man.

I am with a man. He is happy to receive a little car. I believe I am giving it to him. It is small and old and is all dented on both sides, but he is still thrilled. He begins to work on it.

(5) 5/7/03: <u>Title:</u> Two alligators slide out of bag for my wife.

I take a bag into a room where my wife is. The room is long with many windows along the side. I have a big bag. I turn it upside down and an alligator slides out. It is about four or five feet long. She is not afraid. In fact, she wants to play with it. Then a second alligator slides out of the bag. It is about the same size. We are both surprised to see that there are two of them.

(6) 5/8/03: <u>Title:</u> My yellow Cadillac goes down ramp and is threatened to be taken by three men.

I have an older model yellow Cadillac. Somehow I let it go ahead of me and travel on its own. I watch as it heads for a ramp leading downhill to a major highway. It hits the right curb before going down, and I think it will actually just stop there. But it keeps going. It crosses over and hits the left side of the ramp about halfway down. It then crosses over to the right, goes down a bit farther and goes onto the hill on the right and stops. All the time I am running, trying to catch up with it. I then see three men run up and maneuver it down the hill. I assume they think it is a stray car that no one owns—one they can just take. They have parked a large white van on the left side of the access road that

runs parallel to the big highway. I can see that they in-
tend to back the Cadillac up and put it into the van.
The man in front of the car is a thin black man. The
other two are white, I believe. I frantically run down the
ramp, trying to get to them before they take it. I'm not
sure if they will be hostile or not.

In these dreams, you can see a number of images reflecting how
others meet or do not meet the dreamer's expectations. If these were
your dreams, you might begin to see how you are dealing a lot in
these dreams with expectations, fulfilled or anticipated. You might
call this "Cluster A, Expectations in relationships." Within this cluster, you would list the dream references relating to this theme: "Annoyed my family does not do what I expect (1). I have trouble telling
my wife about finding something I did not expect (3). I give a man
something he did not expect; he is happy about it (4). I did not expect my wife to be happy about giving her alligators (5). I don't
know what to expect from strange men (6)."

You can then muse over cluster A, writing something like, "I have
been having trouble lately communicating my expectations to others. Perhaps I am too reserved. I especially seem to have trouble communicating with strangers."

Following this, you might reminisce about previous times you expressed or did not express your desires.

Then you are to write a descriptive paragraph about each element
in the cluster, in chronological order. For example, in the case of
this cluster, you would first write a paragraph about your current
family, or your childhood family, or some family you are familiar
with. The second paragraph would deal with having trouble ex-
plaining something, perhaps including references to your school or
office experiences. And so on through the list.

Finally, you might write a letter to yourself telling about a time when you felt very low, that no one cared about you. But you were surprised when your family presented you with a special gift that you did not expect. You can tell this story and how it affected your life. This is an opportunity to express positive and negative feelings about situations in your life that the dream elements bring up.

Bosnak suggests that you take your time doing these exercises. Set them aside and revisit them later. Try out different genres. Switch the clusters and elements around.

The process can be long and tedious, but what you gain from it can be extremely valuable to you. The point he makes repeatedly is that what you produce from these exercises is not what is most important. "The product you end up with is irrelevant, compared to the change you go through when you seriously set yourself to do this work."[14]

Further capitalization. This step has provided you with insights on how to benefit from your dreams in your waking life by awakening memory of your previous pains and achievements. It is normally a process you would do alone.

Steps 11 and 12, to follow, offer other ways to do this: first by working with others (step 11) and then by going within (step 12). Going within does not necessarily mean you are working "alone." Here you can consciously interact with the characters in your dreams and seek their wisdom.

Another way to gain from your dream insights is by "honoring" the dream. After all the work you have done so far, honoring answers the question, "So, now what?" This aspect of capitalization is so important it deserves a chapter all its own. Chapter 4 offers detailed guidance on how you can benefit from your dreams by honoring them, using the Theme Matrix.

Step 11: Gain from the dream by going outside yourself

This eleventh step has the same characteristics as theme #11 of the Theme Matrix (chapter 2). Here you are integrating your knowledge with other people and other approaches to dream work. You are seeking "truth."

To discover new truths from your dreams, be open to other interpretations. Get input on your dreams from your partner, from a coworker, or from a dream group.

Why seek truth from others about our dreams? It is human nature to be blind to subconscious material. Dreams bring knowledge and information about our true selves to consciousness. This information often suggests change and personal growth. The ego is resistant to change. Even though we may be in pain or going through trials, we normally find it easier to maintain the status quo rather than change the way we are living.

In the face of this personal resistance, others can see things in our dreams that we are not yet willing to face. For instance, suppose you dream that you are back in school and totally unprepared for your final exam. Your subconscious may be trying to warn you that you are failing to prepare for something happening in your home life or work life. It may take a coworker to point out to you that you are about to get in trouble for letting a project slide. You were not crazy about taking on the project in the first place. It may challenge your abilities and call for new training. So you have let preparation for it take a back burner to other, more enjoyable work. Your friend in the office may be noticing that the boss is getting anxious about this project. Your dreams are trying to warn you, but your ego would just as soon hope this project goes away. Your ego doesn't really care to take on new challenges, especially when they require change. It takes another "eye" to suggest what your dream is saying.

With whom should you share? Remember that by sharing a dream with another person, you are revealing your innermost self. Be sure this person is someone you can trust. Normally, it is someone with whom you have built up a relationship over the years. You know this person will keep your conversations confidential. You know this person will respect you and your dreams. You know this person will honor the fact that you consider yourself to be in a growth process—in a continual process of becoming.

If this is the first time you have approached others with a dream, it is a good idea to first inquire about their knowledge of dreams. Do they consider dreams a source of guidance and information? Have they worked with their own dreams or the dreams of others before? By sharing with those who honor dreams, you are assured of getting honest viewpoints about your dream.

Dream groups. When you share your dreams with a group of trusted individuals, you greatly increase your chances of learning what this dream means to you. Each person in the group offers one or more suggestions as to what is "true" for them in this dream. You can then decide for yourself which of their suggestions makes sense for you.

Dreams can have multiple meanings. For instance, a dream about having car trouble may suggest a health problem to one dream group member. Another member may see this dream as dealing with problems in the office. The group may examine all the possible issues regarding cars and other means of transportation and discover insights even they had never "dreamed" of. The act of examination itself is a growth process. Each member of the group learns from the many possibilities suggested by each of the other members.

You may seek out existing groups in the local newspaper or on the Internet. If you cannot find a group in your area, consider starting one yourself. Begin discussing the possibility at your workplace, recreation center, school, or place of worship. You will be surprised how many people you will find who are willing to join.

You will soon learn that the biggest problem starting a group is not getting people to join, but getting people to lead. Most people will say they are not qualified. It is not as scary as you might think. There are excellent books available on how to start and run a dream group. The best of these include the following:

Working with Dreams by Montague Ullman and Nan Zimmerman

Dream Work by Jeremy Taylor

Conscious Dreaming by Robert Moss

As you begin a group, you may want to spend the first hour or so of each meeting reading and discussing the steps in these and other books on dreams. Each member of the group will then take part in the learning process and feel more confident. You may wish to have members take turns leading.

Here are some general tips on running a dream study group. The ideal group size is five to seven people. Be sure the members understand that the group activity is not psychotherapy and is not a substitute for psychotherapy. The group needs to come to agreement on what can be discussed outside the group. Is everything said there to be kept totally confidential, or can things be discussed outside the group so long as anonymity is maintained? Most groups meet weekly or biweekly for about two to three hours. You will probably not be able to thoroughly discuss the dreams of all members in that time, but you should be able to explore one or two in depth. A good practice is to let each member tell a dream, then have the group decide which dreams are to be explored. You might ask, "Who really *needs* to work on a dream?" If no one has a pressing need, the next logical question is "Well, who would *like* to have us work on their dream?"

The following method helps the group to focus on the dream. It is democratic and nonthreatening for the dreamer. It respects the privacy of the dreamer and his or her authority over the dream. Group members need to respect the fact that the dreamer can ask to stop at any point in the process.

First, the dreamer tells the dream, without interruption from the group. Next, the group members can ask any questions of clarification—just about the dream. This is not the time to explore the dreamer's life or his or her thoughts on the dream. Then, group members pretend the dream is their own and reflect on the feelings and activities in the dream as if they were experiencing it themselves. Finally, the dreamer is invited to respond to what the group has said. At this point, the dreamer may wish to include discussion about how the dream is related to waking-life activities or issues. Before leaving the dream, it is good to get some feedback from the dreamer that at least some new insight was gained from this experience.

Books and workshops. It is also good to review your dream using modes presented in other books or in workshops. Many approaches have been presented by authors over the years. There is no one best way for you to examine your dreams. For instance, Margot Born took a dream of her own and showed how it could be approached using seven different methods.[15] Louis M. Savary, Patricia H. Berne, and Strephon Kaplan Williams introduced thirty-seven dream work techniques in their book *Dreams and Spiritual Growth*.[16]

Find a method or suggested approach that you like and work with it for a while. Then try others.

Seek out the available literature. Watch for workshops and retreats in your area. Immerse yourself in the dream world and your dreams will become richer. Seek out the knowledge of others—with the following cautions . . .

There is only one dream "expert." Seeking advice and guidance from others about your dream doesn't mean you are to take their viewpoints as the "meaning" of the dream. Just be aware that these people may offer insights into other possible issues the dream is trying to present and other ways of looking at the dream content.

For instance, beware of the dream dictionary. Remember that the symbol interpretation in the dictionary is just the opinion of one person. Even if you do gain some insight and feel that the particular meaning given for your dream is helpful, keep in mind that the same symbol in your next dream may have an entirely different meaning. If you want to use dream dictionaries and books on symbology, consider what they say as you would the suggestion from a friend or a dream group member. Think of it as something to include in your own examination of the dream. It is not the final word.

Each of us wants and needs to experience our existence in his or her own way. Others can guide and assist, but only the individual can know, understand, and appreciate his or her own teachings and insights.

That's why we emphasize again and again in dream work that you—the dreamer—are the only dream "expert" for your dream. Others can only offer projections of what a dream would mean to them. Legitimately, when others hear your dream, they can only say, "If this were my dream . . ."

Progressive dream journal example. On a separate page or in a separate log or workbook, you might include commentary about new insights you have gained by discussing this with a family member, with a dream group, or through self-examination using a technique from a book or workshop.

6/1/03: Examined the primary symbols in this dream, particularly phone books, bathrooms, and murals.

Asked myself what each of these meant to me. Got
the following insights: . . .

6/11/03: Met with dream group. They had the following additional insights: . . .

Step 12: Capitalize on the dream by going within

This twelfth step has the same characteristics as theme #12 of the
Theme Matrix (chapter 2). Here you are returning to your true
source of wholeness, freedom, and joy. Here you are bringing to conscious realization what is deep within yourself and integrating it with
the surface material—the issues of your waking life. The best way to
do this is through meditation in seclusion and solitude.

Divine guidance. An attendee at one of my dream workshops asked if
dreams came from our subconscious, from the collective unconscious,
or from a divine spirit. My answer was, "Yes! All those sources!"

We are sparks of the divine. We are members of a collective body
of divine sparks. As such, our minds are impressed with divine wisdom that seeks to penetrate to our consciousness so we may better
understand and appreciate the beauty of this existence we have cho-
sen to investigate.

Dreamers are tapping the very core of their inner beings and are
lifting veils to reveal the divine light within. This is "divine guidance." It speaks through your subconscious mind, the collective unconscious, and whatever you consider to be divine. It is as much a
part of you as your body, emotions, and rational mind.

You can also tap into your own source of divine guidance through
meditation.

Meditation. An excellent way of working alone to gain from a
dream's wisdom is through active meditation. In active meditation,

you keep your mind alert. (This is the opposite of passive meditation, which involves attempting to totally still the mind.) Using the
active form of meditation, you are able to get close to the sleep state
but are still able to obtain additional information about the dream
and what it is attempting to offer you.

It is easy for dream work to become a purely mental process.
You may have spent hours poring over the symbols in a dream. You
may have worked through the dream thoroughly with your dream
group. You may have used logical processes to see how the activities
in the dream relate to your waking life. But you still may not fully
understand some aspects of what has happened. You seek further
exploration.

Through active meditation, you can relive the dream. You can re-
experience the feelings in the dream. You can actually carry on a dialogue with the animate and inanimate characters within the dream.

You might say, "Yes, but aren't I just making all this up? When I
am 'talking' to a dream figure, isn't what 'we' are doing really just my
imagination? How can I accept any of this information as valid?"

The classic story we can consider in response to this concern
takes place in a psychotherapist's office. The therapist asks the client
to tell a dream. The client presents this long, involved dream, then
laughs, saying, "I just made all that up." The therapist says, "That
may be, but it came from within you. So let's work with it."

When you go into a semi-altered meditative state, you are getting
closer to the sleep state. What comes to you comes from that deeper
source of knowledge within you. It flows from you with limited inter-
vention from the waking-life mind. The waking-life mind becomes
primarily an observer, a curious reporter.

Understandably, you may still have doubts about the validity of the
information after you have gone through a reliving of the dream or
dialogue with the dream characters. If so, consider the information

you obtain in the same light as you would the information you got from a friend, members of a dream group, or a dream dictionary. How does it feel? Does it make sense? How can I integrate this information with all that I learned from the logical, mental effort I exerted before doing this?

Try it out. Find a place where you can have uninterrupted seclusion and solitude. Light a candle. Sit upright in a chair or on the floor. (If you lie down you are more likely to fall asleep and may not recall what happened.) Close your eyes. Take some deep breaths. Allow yourself to relax and find a place of peace. Then enter the dream as if you were entering a familiar space. Go to any location within the dream. It may be where the dream began. It may not. Walk through the dream locales. What do you see? Do you see anything you did not see before? Whom do you meet? Approach anything and anyone you feel can offer information about the questions that you have about the dream. Ask them questions such as "Who are you?" and "Why are you wearing that outfit?" Ask anything about which you do not have complete understanding. Wait for their response. Continue the dialogue for as long as you wish.

When you feel you have gone through as much of the dream as you feel is necessary, bring yourself slowly back to waking life. This is best initiated by wiggling your toes and tapping your fingers. Open your eyes gently and gradually.

You may want to have pen and paper ready to record as much as you can recall. As you become more experienced with this, you may find you can actually record activities and conversations while you are in the meditative state.

You might want to consider this meditation to be a whole new dream. Go through the step-by-step process of evaluation as you did with the original dream. What emotions did you feel? Were there emotions you did not feel that you believe you should have felt?

Can you give this meditation a title? A theme? Are these different from those attributed to the original dream? Did you learn anything you did not know before? Does what you learned offer new information you can use in your waking life?

Be open to the next question, the next adventure, the next dream. What is the next step in dealing with the issue or issues you have confronted in the dream and the meditation? What new questions do you have? What questions are still unanswered? Begin to form questions you would like addressed in your next dream.

Active meditation is a fruitful way to gain information about your dream. Through this you tap the higher consciousness you possess within yourself.

Personal example. In place of the progressive dream journal example that has followed each previous step, we will close with a very personal example of the active meditation process. It is personal because the dream I am about to relate is perhaps one of the most important dreams of my life. I feel dreams are sacred, so I am reluctant to share some of my more intimate, major ones. But I feel it was the meditation experience that gave this dream its true significance. I'm not sure I would have caught the true essence of the dream without the subsequent meditation. It's a rather long dream, so I will just present the last part, which inspired my meditation:

> A man leads me through a building. I follow him down some steps. He stops at the entrance to a long, covered walkway. Another man thanks me for having come. He walks ahead with who I believe is a prince. I am glad I have no shoes on because the two men walking ahead of me have taken theirs off. They may have socks on. At some point, either at the beginning of a corridor or at

the end, I see a small round wafer dipped in something. I may have been offered it. A small boy asks for one but is denied by a man who says the boy wants them too much, like it is wine or something and bad for the boy. The boy does not see the real meaning behind the wafer and wine, only the good taste. At the end of the corridor, which has a green carpet, the two men seem to have disappeared. I come to a large apartment. There is a big room off to the left where a lot of food is being laid out. Straight ahead is a Christmas tree. A young girl, I believe dressed in blue, is standing in the tree. She is partly covered by the branches. She may have been in front of the tree at first. But as I look at her, I see her in among the branches. I see her face closely. She may have talked to me, but all I recall is a tear on her left cheek. I think it is a glass or crystal tear placed on her cheek. I ask, "How may I help you?"

This dream raised many questions for me. I was just beginning a whole new phase of my life, filled with change upon change. I knew I was involved in a spiritual reawakening. At the time, I was immersing myself in literature and lectures in which so-called prophets were predicting what I considered to be dire circumstances for the planet. I was beginning to doubt the chances of my own survival and the survival of humanity. I was guided by members of my dream group to go within and seek answers from my inner guides—the higher consciousness from which dreams originate.

Since the girl in the Christmas tree lived in this space of high consciousness, I decided to address my questions to her. Following is the general narrative of the key points in my meditation:

"Does this apartment belong to the prince?" "*Yes.*"

"Is the prince the Prince of Peace?" "*Yes.*"

"What does the Christmas tree signify?" "*The Christmas tree is representative of the future, influenced by the physical, emotional, and spiritual changes taking place within the planet and within humanity. The planet is taking on an initiation of sorts, and all will be affected.*"

"What is the significance of the tear coming down your cheek, and why do I see it as both glass and crystal?" "*You can choose to see the new changes coming about as disastrous and horrible, represented by the glass tear of sorrow. Or you can choose to see the changes as beautiful and divine, represented by the crystal tear, a tear of joy. The choice is yours to make.*"

———

And you, too, now have choices to consider. You have just examined your dream in great detail within this twelve-step process. You hopefully have a better understanding of what the issues are in your life and the questions you need to address.

In summary, you examined your dream by following the steps offered in this chapter:

1. **Recording the events and emotions of your day.**
   Maintain a dream journal, a running log of your dream life. Include the events and emotions of the day.

2. **Recording the theme or themes of the day.**
   One practice that may help you do this is to recall how you received a blessing, a challenge, and an opportunity to serve each day.

3. **Recording the dream from your sleep period.**
   Capture whatever you recall. To keep the dream fresh and alive, it is best to write it in the present tense.

4. **Determining the emotions and feelings found within the dream and your emotions on waking.**
   Record emotions you or other characters displayed in the dream, emotions or feelings you would expect to be expressed in the dream but are not expressed, and your emotions on waking.

5. **Determining a title for the dream.**
   Write it like a newspaper headline, addressing the who, what, when, and where questions.

6. **Determining a theme for the dream.**
   Determining the theme requires that you deal with the real-life issue the dream is trying to present.

7. **Interacting with the dream theme by relating it to the Theme Matrix.**
   Finding the core theme that best relates to the theme of your dream leads you to deeper understanding of the question your subconscious mind is asking you to investigate.

8. **Interacting with the theme by relating it to the theme(s) of the day.**
   Ask yourself where in your waking life you are acting out or being presented with this theme.

9. **Interacting with the theme of the dream by relating it to other dreams.**
   Maintain a list of your dream titles and themes to find re-curring themes.

10. **Benefiting from the dream by reminiscing on dream themes.**
    Revisit your dreams using activities that lessen conscious control, such as poetry or dance. Muse or reminisce on recurring themes.

11. **Gaining from the dream by going outside yourself, getting input from others.**
    Get input on your dreams from a trusted partner, dream literature, or a dream group.

12. **Capitalizing on the dream by going within, getting input from meditation.**
    Tap into the subconscious, the collective unconscious, and whatever you consider divine.

But where do you go from here? In the final chapter to follow, you are offered a method of moving beyond the dream. Again making use of the core themes in the Theme Matrix, you will be shown how to benefit from your dream by examining the next phase of your journey, moving to a higher level of consciousness. This is called "honoring" the dream.

four

Honoring the Dream

> *No problem can be solved*
> *from the same level of*
> *consciousness that created it.*
> —ALBERT EINSTEIN

Themes and the Theme Matrix help you to explore your dream. They help you zero in on an issue or concern you are dealing with—or being led by your dreams to deal with—in your life. This is something your dream is attempting to bring to your consciousness. The Theme Matrix also offers suggestions on how to benefit from the message the dream is presenting. This is called "honoring" your dream. Honoring moves you beyond the dream. It leads you to the next question. Honoring asks you to be open to what the dream suggests for change and transformation.

This concept builds on Jeremy Taylor's second basic assumption that "No dream comes just to tell the dreamer what he or she already knows."[17] Even recurring dreams have some element in them that leads us on to the next question, the next phase of the journey.

For example, in step 9 of chapter 3, we examined several dreams that dealt with expression of will. Although they all shared some commonality with this theme, each dream expressed the theme in a different way, offering unique insight into the issue. One dream presented the dreamer's annoyance at not having wishes or desires met. But another dream offered a suggestion on how to deal with this. It showed the dreamer that through persistence and determination, one's desires could be fulfilled. Yet another dream in this series presented a new twist on the issue. It said that through willful exploration you may find something you did not expect; in this case it posed a possible threat. Each dream adds some new piece of information that can be useful in service to our health and wholeness.

The point is that we cannot just take a dream for granted and write it off as "just a dream." If we do this, we will be inclined to ignore the dream. We may say, "Oh, that's another one of those 'expressing will' dreams. I have those all the time." We will then miss the next piece of valuable information our dreams are trying to tell us.

As with each waking event in our lives, each dream is a step toward the future, a phase of the journey of life. Dreams come to us to drive us forward.

This chapter shows you how to move forward to the next step. How to benefit from your dreams. How to honor your dreams. You begin by thinking at a higher level of consciousness.

Levels of consciousness

Esoteric teachings state that our personalities are essentially composed of three levels of consciousness that relate to the degree of density of matter.

The most dense of these is the physical level—the body. As a level of consciousness, this represents our more animalistic, instinctual nature. We experience this consciousness through our five physical senses. For instance, it is here that we feel pain and pleasure, hunger and satiety.

Less dense is our astral body—our emotional consciousness. This is the level at which we experience nonphysical feelings such as joy, sadness, enthusiasm, anticipation, guilt, fear, and love.

Next is the mental body. It is through the mind that we are able to think and reason. The mind allows us to understand abstract concepts and patterns. At this level of consciousness, we can use our imagination to create.

Above the physical, astral, and mental levels there are higher, less dense levels of consciousness. For our purposes we will call these levels "spiritual."

The esoteric teachings go on to say that we can resolve issues arising at one level of consciousness by concentrating our energies on the next higher level of consciousness. For instance, if you are physically impaired in some way—perhaps immobilized—it helps to seek pastimes that bring you joy. You might find a new hobby, watch old comedy movies, or immerse yourself in music or literature. By doing this, you avoid victim mentality and can accept the fact that you are more than just your physical body.

If you experience an emotional loss, such as the breakup of a relationship, you can rise above feelings of depression and anxiety by seeking mental diversions. You may engross yourself in your work. Or you might sign up for a class. By doing this, again you avoid victim mentality and can accept the fact that you are more than just your emotions. If you find yourself overtaxed mentally, you may seek approaches that are considered spiritual. These would include meditation, peaceful music, inspirational reading or writing—any approach that will calm the mind.

Raising your level of consciousness is the most healthy way to resolve any issue. It keeps you from stagnating or, worse yet, allowing yourself to sink lower. And it helps you to see that you are more than your body, more than your emotions, more than your thoughts.

In chapter 2, we noted that the core themes of the Theme Matrix can also be treated as phases in our life journey. We gain new insights from each new experience. We achieve new consciousness, new awareness. We lift a veil, so to speak, to reveal new insights, enabling us to operate at higher levels of consciousness as we deal with the issues we are facing. Using the Theme Matrix as a model of progression, we can apply the practice of concentrating on subsequent themes—advanced phases, "higher" levels—to resolve current issues presented in our dreams. The procedure that follows can help you benefit from, or honor, your dreams by using the Theme Matrix as this progressive model.

How to honor your dream

Following are suggested actions to take when faced with issues at each level in the model. Note that this procedure treats the core themes in the Theme Matrix as phases of progression in life and as levels of consciousness. Each suggestion prompts you to investigate the *next* phase or level in the matrix and initiate actions recommended at that level. (For example, you would use theme #2 actions to deal with a dream that has all the elements of theme #1.) Taking these actions is a way of honoring the dream by honoring its theme.

Honoring personal identity (theme #1) issues

When faced with issues of personal identity, assert your will and personal power, taking actions that fulfill personal needs, improve your possessions, or otherwise improve your sense of material security.

Self-identity, vulnerability, and your outlook on life are key issues of core theme #1. Acting on core theme #2 issues supplies you with the tools needed to know yourself. When your material needs are met, you begin to become more self-reliant, create a better outlook on life, and improve your self-image. Embrace these elements when your dreams or events in your life make you question your self-image or outlook on life. As an example, consider the following dream:

> I am outdoors in a village of some sort. I am with a woman who takes me to cement steps leading down. But I notice they only go down seven or eight steps and not all the way to the ground, which is still quite a ways below. I also notice a weakness in them. I hold on to the handrail to my right and try to move the steps with my feet without falling. I finally work several of the lower steps loose, and they go crashing to the ground below.

This dream has to do with vulnerability and safety, consistent with core theme #1. This might remind you of those times in the past when you felt vulnerable or alone. When this happened, your outlook on life perhaps diminished. You had a low sense of self-worth. Perhaps the dream is bringing to light these feelings from your current waking-life situation.

Note that in the dream you have a handrail—some element of security to help you in this situation. In your waking-life situation, you might think of "handrails" available to you. You do have material security, and you have the power to use what is at your disposal. Also, you do not fall in the dream. You hold on. You hold your ground. You are no longer able to proceed in the direction you were led, but you are unharmed and able to find another way.

Honoring personal resources (theme #2) issues

When faced with issues relating to personal resources, security, or self-reliance, take actions that stretch your thought capabilities, improve your functioning capability, and enable you to communicate.

Self-reliance and personal security are key issues of core theme #2. Acting on core theme #3 issues helps you increase your personal power and self-reliance. Thinking things out and setting new goals help you to become less dependent on others for your physical and psychological security. Communicating your thoughts to others helps you learn interdependence. The following dream provides an example of this issue:

> I am finishing up a meal with some friends. We all start to get up to leave. I stay at the table because I want to finish my wine. I am the only one having wine. I take my glass to the exit. I quickly finish the last of my wine and put the glass on a shelf or tray. The others have gone on ahead. When I get outside, I think I see them way down at the corner to the far left, so I hurry to catch up. I think I see them go into a club down there, so I go in a side entrance, hoping to intercept them. Inside, I head to the left and walk all the way through the place, but I don't see them. I come back and walk the other way. At some point, a pretty girl, sitting at a table with a guy, looks up at me and gives me the eye. I feel she is attracted to me. When I cannot find the guys, I think of going back and trying to connect with her.

This is a dream that might raise issues of abandonment. The friends have gone off without waiting. You might have feelings they were actually trying to get away from you. But you pursue. You become self-reliant. You use your reasoning ability to avoid victim mentality. You create a plan in your mind of an alternative to what looks like abandonment. The alternative solution—connecting with the pretty girl—involves a certain level of skill at communication. This dream has all the elements of theme #2 issues being dealt with through theme #3 actions.

One point of caution if you are facing this issue in waking life: be sure not to let the pretty girl become a crutch. Remember that you are seeking continued "interdependence," not dependence.

A personal note: Recently, someone I was close to raised in me old childhood issues of abandonment. I treated this issue as a waking dream and consulted the Theme Matrix for suggestions on what to do. The theme the issue presented dealt with my need for personal security and self-reliance. By examining the next theme level in the matrix, I realized the only way to really resolve this issue was to communicate my concerns to that person. I began to understand that what I was going through was caused solely by my feelings and was not any fault of the other person. This helped me maintain a close relationship that might otherwise have been jeopardized.

Honoring issues of self-reliance and personal security can best be dealt with by concentrating your efforts at the next higher level of consciousness. This involves thought. It involves activity which enables "functioning"—forward mobility.

Honoring personal thought (theme #3) issues

When faced with issues relating to processing, synthesizing and communicating thought, take actions that express your true feelings, finding ways to be compassionate, nurturing, and care-giving to yourself and to others.

Your ability to function well in your environment and communicate your thoughts are key elements of core theme #3. Working with core theme #4 "feeling" actions helps you to set realistic goals and develop strategies, thus functioning without being too much "in your head."

The following dream deals with the issue of communication:

> I am trying to reach someone for help. I use my mobile phone, but I just get a long commercial pitch from a woman. It is probably just a recording, but nothing I would expect on my mobile phone.

Telephone malfunction is a common dream experienced throughout the world. The problem need not be with the machine itself. It could indicate a waking-life issue of not being able to communicate with others easily. If this rings true with you, you might want to examine the degree to which you express your true feelings to others.

This dream also raises the telemarketer issue. You might need to think of how you deal with others who impose on your time. Can you communicate your feelings about this thoughtfully and with reason? Can you control your feelings? Can you be levelheaded? Compassionate about their feelings?

Many times we get so caught up in the mental processes going on in our heads that we forget to consider the feelings of others. And, perhaps more importantly, we don't zero in on our own feelings about how we are treating others. Getting in touch with feelings is a great way to get out of one's head.

Many homes these days are constructed within feet of other homes, allowing for little privacy. If you are in one of these homes, you may decide to plant some tall trees or hedges to form a wall separating you from a too-close neighbor. You can perform research on heights and widths and growing times of trees. Based on this, you can plan where and when to plant them. But suppose your neighbor has just planted a vegetable garden on the other side of your fence. Your well-thought-out plan may block the sun from this garden. Staying in "mental mode" alone, without considering the feelings of and communicating with all those concerned, may create more problems than you started with. Facing your neighbor and speaking your true feelings takes great courage and discipline.

Honoring expression of feelings and compassion (theme #4) issues

When faced with issues relating to feelings, compassion, nurturing, and caregiving, take actions that truly express your will, enabling you to develop creativity and passion for new discoveries.

Compassion, caring, and sensitivity are key issues of core theme #4. Working with personal will and power—actions at the fifth theme level—helps you understand and improve compassion for yourself and others.

Consider the following dream:

> I have gotten myself some food and take it to a table
> that has been saved for me. I can see a seashell sitting on
> the table, indicating the table is mine. But a large man
> that I know from dream conferences is now sitting at
> the table. There is not really enough room for me to sit
> across from him, but I try. I have to pull the table out a
> bit to try to squeeze in. There is a man sitting at the
> table to the left who tries to help me make room.

The theme of this dream is *Someone is intruding on my space.* It deals with core theme #4 issues regarding caring for the feelings of others. There is an old axiom that you cannot love someone else until you love yourself. Loving one's self means being true to one's own will. If you feel someone is intruding on your space—not caring about your feelings—you need to stand up for what you believe. The lesson here might be the reverse. You may need to look at yourself and see if you are the one intruding, not caring. Every character in the dream can be seen as an aspect of yourself. The lesson may be the reverse of what it appears to be in the dream.

Another aspect of being truthful with yourself deals with seeking out what truly brings you joy and passion—what makes you want to get up in the morning. Knowing this and living this will make you a better nurturer and caregiver for another.

Suppose you are placed in a position of having to care for someone dear to you. You might begin to find yourself facing issues concerning the sacrifice of your personal freedom. Are you missing out on things that bring you joy? Is the sacrifice you are making worth it? Is the person you are caring for taking advantage of you? You will need to come to grips with these issues. You will need to come to an understanding within yourself that your personal will and power are not being diminished. At that point, nurturing, compassion, and caregiving will be a joyful, fulfilling experience.

Honoring expression of will (theme #5) issues

When faced with issues relating to exerting personal will through creativity, exploration, and discovery, take actions that improve personal analytical skills, looking for ways to improve the service work you do on the job or seeking new challenges.

Deciding what you want and taking action to fulfill your desires are key issues of core theme #5. Working with theme #6 actions improves your creativity and decisiveness. Developing your analytical skills provides you with more options. You are able to take more creative approaches to every new idea or adventure in life when you have the appropriate skills. You also can be of better service to others. You are more adaptable and thus can meet new challenges with confidence.

As an example, suppose you had the following dream:

> I go up to a room. I want to experiment with painting pictures. Instead of creating any of my own, I begin touching up two paintings that belong to someone else. One is a picture of a house with little yellow dots down near the bottom, perhaps on steps. I mess with it and begin just sweeping my paintbrush back and forth across it. Then I see that I have totally obliterated the picture. What have I done? This is not even my picture to mess with. I try to clean it off and think I see the original house but with another house in white to the left of it. I go back downstairs hoping something can be done about it.

The theme of this dream might be *I am destroying another's possessions*. It is related to core theme #5 because the dreamer is expressing his or her will over that of others. Even before the dream is over, the dreamer is attempting to think of analytical ways of dealing with this situation.

If you had this dream and it brought you to the realization that you are engaged in similar activity in your waking life, the best way to resolve it is by using your analytical skills. For instance, if you are bringing harm to another, you may look for ways to serve that person in a more positive way. If you are seeking creative expression by just copying the work or style of others, you may seek ways to develop your own approach. You may need to sign up for special training to develop your skills.

Taking action to improve your skills and abilities helps develop self-confidence and ignites your creative juices.

Honoring expression of analytical skills (theme #6) issues

When faced with issues relating to your personal analytical skills and developing confidence to meet challenges, take actions that involve uniting in a relationship or partnership and balance with a person, cause, place, or work endeavor.

Self-confidence is a key issue of core theme #6. Uniting with others helps you develop this in core theme #7. The best way to truly improve your skills and ensure you know how to meet challenges well is to find ways to share your talents and aspirations with another. This may be in a love relationship or a business partnership.

For example, assume you are having trouble completing a project at work or at home because you lack a particular skill. The quickest way to move forward is to get someone else involved who is able to lead you in the right direction. By uniting with another in such a partnership, you improve your skill level. This has the added benefit of building your confidence.

You might have to "eat crow" a bit, admitting that you are not proficient in every challenge placed before you. In this respect, the key word to keep in mind is "balance." Dancers know that when one partner tries to control too much or is a "limp rag," the couple is out of balance. What could be an enjoyable, pleasant dance can turn out to be a painful struggle. Every relationship has this element of give and take, requiring humility and respect for one's partner.

You might enjoy the following "story" dream, in which the dreamer helps the key figure in the dream. It is an example of using one's skills to avoid danger. But saving the "hero" also involves working in partnership.

I am observing something like a story about a man who swings from ropes and vines. I somehow know he is to go to a long vine that is in the courtyard to make an escape. But I see him here in another, more enclosed area. He is getting away from bad guys. He looks up at these vines right here and sees they are broken and cut short. So he begins to run away through rooms that have nuts and acorns all over the floor. He needs to be careful to avoid them. He goes to the other side of the building. He never makes it to the courtyard in the middle of the building. He goes to a large, crowded room. He is not sure what to do next. Then I turn a crank at a large picture window that opens it from both ends. It is as if the window turns on an axis in the middle. The man is then able to escape to an open area. A Chasidic festival is going on out there, and he joins in. I see him much later when it is dark, slowly walking up a hill and away from the place. I guess the bad guys never got him.

Honoring balance and partnership (theme #7) issues

When faced with issues relating to partnership, love, and balance, take actions that involve sharing resources and desires, sharing personal will and power, or expressing yourself through others.

Key issues of core theme #7 are love and commitment. A relationship can become more balanced when you can let go of your personal attachment to "things" and see them as belonging to the partnership. Involving yourself with core theme #8 activity helps you put more of your total self into the partnership.

We come into relationships with our own baggage. This baggage is not just in the form of material possessions. It includes our experience in former relationships. It includes our prejudices. It includes what we have learned to love and what we can barely tolerate. Sharing our baggage with that of another person in an intimate relationship means giving up some of our personal will—some of our power.

An example of this was given in the discussion under theme #2. In this case, I explained how I grew up with issues of abandonment. Deep-seated feelings about issues such as these may last a lifetime. These feelings may stay dormant when one is alone. But when that person enters into a relationship, they can surface at the slightest provocation. By sharing this old baggage with your partner, you may be surprised to find he or she shares the same issues.

We each have visions about our plans for the future. Marriage counselors advise anyone going into a lifelong relationship to be sure they have a clear idea of the visions and desires of the other person. If your visions differ, how much of your will and power are you willing to "share" to keep the relationship in balance? Sharing vision may mean giving up some of your personal power. But doing so strengthens the commitment you have made with the other person to live in balance as partners.

The following dream shows how we can bring things into balance by offering up what we have. In this case, the shared resource is service.

> My wife and I are finishing up working at a place. We have built a short wall made up of five or six square pillars. It is unpainted—a light-colored wood. I see some other older square pillars standing around. My wife says something about our forgetting to do something. I think she means that we need to check these older pillars to see if they are stable. But then she points to this smaller structure resting on top of a pillar. It is sort of

leading back onto something else. It is perhaps a clock or narrow statue. We are supposed to get that down and move it. We are about to do that when a round-faced woman has someone else do it. She seems to be in charge or taking charge. We are grateful she did this for us. I then go to this kitchen at the far end. I think I'm about done with my work here and am checking things over. But I see that others have left a mess here, so I need to clean up more. A man comes and is pleased with what I am doing.

The dreamer and his partner are ready and willing to fulfill a previously arranged obligation when another comes and completes it for them. Instead of just leaving, the dreamer then fulfills someone else's obligation. This is a form of "paying forward." The dreamer is perhaps being called upon to seek ways of working in balance in his waking life, not just with his immediate partner, but with others as well. The dream is suggesting he do this by sharing his energy in service even when not obligated to do so. He is learning to seek balance in his interactions on a broader societal scale.

Honoring shared resources (theme #8) issues

When faced with issues relating to sharing resources while fulfilling personal desires, take actions that involve thinking from the other person's perspective. Consider the future of the relationship rather than the momentary feelings or reactions.

A primary lesson involved in core theme #8 is learning how to share. Working with activities at the core theme #9 level helps you to share while still being true to your own wishes. By thinking from the perspective of others and learning to adapt to the changing situations they create for you, you improve your sharing skills. This is basic human psychology and the basis for most conflict resolution today.

One of the best examples of this concept is the mediation process. If you are having a disagreement with a partner in a business or personal relationship, a key step in mediation is to have you explain the other person's point of view. By expressing what you believe the other person is saying, you are engaging in an act of sharing. You are seeking to fully understand the desires and will of the other. This is true interaction.

Consider the following dream:

> I look out the window in the door and see a workman in blue walking up our driveway. Then I see more of the workmen coming up. I feel it is the stonemason and his crew and that they have come up with a quick solution for our wall and patio problems. I seem to recall him saying something about it earlier, but am surprised to see he actually has a plan. I see what I think is a small model of a structure that they have set up in the parking area. Then I am out there looking back toward the entrance. My wife and I had put up part of a semicircle as an entryway. These guys have added to it by putting up a cheap plastic wall to the left. It is all very crude and quite ugly. I then see a large round object in the parking area with a large star attached to the front of it. I go around to the street side of the house where they have constructed several large structures. One has a castle-like design across the top edge. It is all very crude.

The theme of this dream is *Getting something we don't want or like*. It deals with theme #8 issues in that it relates to joint resources (the dreamer's house) and joint desires (what the dreamer and his wife thought they wanted). However, the perspective of the one hired to do the work appears to be quite different. If all the characters in the dream are parts of the dreamer, perhaps the dream indicates an issue concerning joint perspectives in waking life. Perhaps in some aspect of the dreamer's life, information was not shared beforehand on a joint project. Perhaps the dream calls for mediation at this point.

Honoring adaptation and perspective (theme #9) issues

When faced with issues relating to adapting or broadening your perspective through conceptualized thought, take actions that involve using what you have accomplished in your life to help others heal, transform, and experience renewal.

A key issue of core theme #9 is responsibility. By working with activities at the core theme #10 level, you learn to assume responsibility for life. By thinking in terms of what is good for humanity, you broaden your perspective and are better able to interact responsibly in your immediate personal relationships.

Consider the following dream:

> I am working in a large store, perhaps a health food store. One guy has to leave for a while and I fill in for him. While he is gone, this girl asks me to talk to her boyfriend on the phone. The boyfriend asks if he can have a truckload of this particular candy. I say yes. He is very grateful and asks if he can give me something for my generosity. I begin to think that he really needs to pay for all this candy. He thinks I am just going to give it to him. Perhaps I was just caught up in the mechanics of being able to get all this on a truck, not the practical

part about cost. I think I can perhaps offer him a discount on part of it. While I am involved in this, someone tells me I have another call way over on the other side of this place. I'm annoyed that I have to go all the way over there. I should be able to have the call transferred. When I get back, the other guy has returned. He tells me he cancelled the whole deal with the boyfriend. I'm relieved that we didn't get stuck.

The dreamer here is involved in a business partnership and is asked to take on some additional responsibility. The boyfriend is perhaps trying to take advantage of him while the one in charge is away. The theme of this dream is *Doing business without fully thinking about the consequences*. It is related to core theme #9 because it involves taking responsibility and dealing with opportunity. The concepts of core theme #10 involve helping others. But it is important to note that by helping we need to use wisdom and consider the "common good." The dreamer must not only consider the desires of the boyfriend, but also what is appropriate as a member of the business team. He considers offering a discount as compensation, but perhaps is not in a position to do this. If this is related to a waking-life pattern, perhaps the dreamer needs to broaden his perspective by applying what he has learned for the general good.

Honoring applied learning (theme #10) issues

When faced with issues relating to applying what you have learned to benefit yourself and society, take actions that involve humanitarianism, community-mindedness, nonattachment, and commitment to universal truths.

Core theme #10 deals with applying the wisdom you have gained. Involving yourself with core theme #11 actions broadens your outlook.

Community-mindedness and commitment to truth are key elements of core theme #11. They help you to use what you have learned for the general good.

An example of an issue you may face in this respect has to do with ego. It is easy to get caught up in feelings of self-importance because of the honors thrust upon us based on our accomplishments. On the other hand, we may lose self-esteem by dwelling on honors we feel are due to us that were not received. In either case, we are so caught up in "self" that we may forget our responsibility to humanity and the continuity of life in general.

By engaging in community activity and continually attempting to understand and live by universal truths, we can remain centered on healing and transformation of humanity in general.

As an example, consider the following dream:

> I am with a group of people who have been chastised
> and forced to be separate somehow. We are at a large
> resort. I go around to the other side of this place where
> most of the people are. I climb a sandy hill and stand
> up, facing out. There are people behind me and others
> gathered out ahead of me at lower levels. I feel like I am
> a spokesman for our group, one who needs to mediate
> and help heal things. I stand and raise up my arms.
> Someone in charge behind me quiets the crowd and
> says we need to listen to what I have to say. I look
> around and shout out, "You are the light of the world.
> Rumi said that his eyes are small but they see wondrous
> things. You are the light of the world. You can see won-
> drous things. We have entertainment for you on the
> other side of the hill."[18] I then leave and go to the other
> side. I believe people come to see us. Later I go back

around to this side again and see that a man there has
begun singing and entertaining as well. He is sitting in
a bar. He gets out different drinks and setups as part of
his act. I help him.

In this dream, the dreamer recognizes that there are people who
are in need of help. We do not know why they are oppressed. Perhaps it is because they have beliefs that are not accepted by the general populace. The dreamer feels called upon to express a truth he
learned from a wise person. The intent is to "enlighten" people that
they are not wrong for what they believe.

If this were your dream, perhaps the dream is asking you to serve
the public by offering knowledge you have gained—perhaps through
your own chastisement and separation. The vehicle for this is to be
some form of entertainment. Perhaps an artistic endeavor. Perhaps
you are to write a book or screenplay. By taking such action in waking life, you honor theme #10 issues (healing and transformation)
through theme #11 action (community-mindedness and commitment to truth). The dream is presenting the issue and offering a suggestion for action.

Honoring truth and value (theme #11) issues

*When faced with issues relating to what you know to be truly essential
and of value, take actions that enable you to realize the freedom your
beliefs give you to make choices that enable you to seek wholeness, true
joy, and spontaneity.*

The key issues of core theme #11 are nonattachment and commitment to truth. By going inward, engaging in activities at level #12,
we gain a clearer understanding of what these concepts mean. With
this understanding comes the freedom to choose how we use the

power of our truth in community. It is then easier to let go of petty desires and illusions and accept ourselves as part of the whole.

Consider the following rather disturbing dream:

> I am with a man and woman. Somehow we are all involved in the murder of anther man and woman. I watch as the woman strangles the other woman. The man apparently has already killed the man. I seem to just watch, without emotion, almost anxious that it be finished. Later, I am in an enclosed area that seems to be outdoors. Others know that these murders have happened and are looking around for clues. I help them look, although I know where we have buried the evidence. They look just inside this area, but I know there are things buried just under the fence or hedge area right along the edge of this place. Someone asks, "How could anyone kill them?" I don't respond but keep looking. I begin to think about the woman who was killed and feel some remorse. I realize that I really liked her. Why did I not do anything to stop this? I seemed to be frozen in place as it happened, unable to do anything.

A possible theme for this dream would be *I am involved in major wrongdoing*. It is a dream about theme #11 issues. The dream deals with the dreamer's state of mind regarding basic lessons learned about life and truth, lessons thought to be already integrated, lessons about events thought to be beyond the realm of possibility. The dreamer is obviously being confronted with what he or she believes to be truly essential or of value in society. There is concern about continuity of life in general. But the more vital issue is the personal torment felt by the dreamer concerning subjugation of personal power. He or she is "frozen," unable to act in response to a clear violation of universal truth. Community acceptance is threatened. Identity with the group is threatened.

Core theme #12, the next "life cycle" level, deals with making choices concerning your beliefs. When dreams or waking-life experiences cause you to question your value structure, or when you feel powerless to act or speak out on behalf of what you know to be true, it is time to go within to examine your beliefs. The intensity of a dream such as this indicates that you are dealing with some pretty heavy stuff—stuff worthy of self-examination. The dream suggests that you go "inside"—inside the area where the "evidence" is hidden. Core theme #12 action involves going into seclusion and meditating on what you believe about maintaining life and concealing truth.

Another way to work with these issues is to go into a meditative state and dialogue with the characters in the dream. A prime candidate for inquiry is the woman we actually witness committing a murder. Why is the woman strangling the other woman? Why is she not using some other means? If you consider her to be an aspect of your own character, you might inquire as to what this woman feels needs to be suffocated and made lifeless. Some old illusions or desires? The dream seems to involve boundary issues. Why was the evidence buried exactly at the boundary of this nondescript enclosed place? Can the frozen, remorseful dream character—you—or the actual murderers answer this? What could the evidence be? Are the bodies missing?

Going within to seek truth releases you from attachments to illusions and petty desires and helps you to realize what you know to be true for yourself and your existence within the "community" of humanity.

Honoring freedom and wholeness (theme #12) issues

When faced with issues involving your beliefs about freedom from limitations, making choices, and being grounded and in control, take actions that involve differentiating your self-image, self-identity, and your outlook on life—all attributes of theme #1.

The key elements of core theme #12 are freedom and spontaneity. By taking appropriate action, you can learn to live joyously in the moment and experience spontaneity and freedom. You can perhaps find happiness through others. You can perhaps find happiness and contentment in the search for truth. But joy, freedom, and spontaneity can only come through true acceptance and love of yourself and your beliefs.

The life cycle journey does not end when you come to theme #12. Progression onward involves returning to core theme #1. You have come full circle through the themes and are ready to begin the cycle anew. Life is an unending adventure, a quest for the grail, an open invitation to the next dream. As you complete a round of the life cycle, you are ready for a new adventure and lessons at higher levels of consciousness. Think of the life cycle as a spiral, with each step at a higher level than the last. Step 1 on your new cycle is actually at a higher level than step 12 on the cycle you just completed. So your next "higher" level theme issues involve engaging yourself in level #1 activity, that is, looking at your self-identity and your outlook on life.

The dream we examined in the previous section—an example of honoring theme #11 issues—related to making choices about beliefs and values. The freedom of the dreamer is threatened because of what he or she did not do to prevent a murder. The dreamer is unable to live joyously in the moment. If this were your dream, you may need to think about your belief system as an expression of yourself. Are you free to be yourself? To express what you believe?

Another aspect of core theme #12 issues involves recognizing your limitations. Perhaps you have had a dream similar to the following:

> I am moving into a desk at my office. Perhaps I am returning to an office I had been in years ago. It is very crowded here. I learn they had to compress space to allow for more desks. We have been allotted only so many. We are to all take our places so they can see if we have enough space or if we need to ask to take over spaces at other desks. I settle in at my space. I am sitting with my back to the aisle. I pick up a metal container and see it is full of trash. There is nothing in it of any use to me, so I dump it in the trash can. Soon another man comes to my desk and sits by the wall facing in to my right. The desk is against the wall, and I guess we have to allow for three people at each desk. This is not just my desk, as I had thought.

In this dream, you are presented with limitations. You "settle in," recognizing that you are a part of a community. This is a suggestion to look at your outlook on life. In the dream, you get rid of someone else's trash. This is a suggestion to take a look at how you differentiate yourself from others. In the dream, you are called upon to consider what is "my desk." This is asking, "What is my self-identity?"—a question asked in core theme #1.

Dreams may or may not make obvious suggestions for taking action at the next level. But in your attempts to honor dreams, it is a good idea to seek what they offer. At any rate, involving yourself in activities suggested by the next core theme will help you benefit from your dreams.

———

This chapter culminates your introduction to themes and how they can serve you in dream life and in waking life. Dreams are enriching experiences. Each dream is a new adventure in itself and another step on the path of the grand adventure.

Each new dream lifts a veil. Look deeply into its eyes. Partake of its wisdom. Bathe in the new question it poses. Lose yourself in the mystery and find the true self that lies within you.

Sweet dreams.

appendix a

Summary of
the Theme Matrix
Characteristics

DIFFERENTIATION

Themes based on how you differentiate yourself from others

Theme	Motivation	Life issues, aspects, fields of activity	Blessing/challenge	Honor the dream by
1: What is your personal self-image? Who are you?	Issues dealing with sensitivity, caring, love, or applied wisdom	Self-identity—your perception about how you look and appear before the world. Outlook on life—your expectations about being accepted by others, and the degree to which you feel accepted by others. Vulnerability—susceptibility to being injured, attacked, or criticized. Your feelings of vulnerability lead you to seek physical, emotional, and mental safety and protection.	Self-acceptance/ nonacceptance	asserting your will and personal power and taking actions that fulfill personal needs, improve your possessions, or otherwise improve your sense of material security.
2: What personal resources do you have and need for security and self-reliance?	Issues dealing with will, determination, or use of power	Possessions—your material possessions, capabilities, and financial resources. Self-reliance—the ability to provide for yourself physically and emotionally. Power and energy—the strength and endurance needed to control your actions.	Needs satisfied/ needs not satisfied	taking actions that stretch your thought capabilities, improve your functioning capability, and enable you to communicate.
3: How do you synthesize and communicate personal thought?	Issues dealing with thought, reason, or adaptability	Thinking—your ability to reason and synthesize thought, enabling you to function in your environment. Environment—your day-to-day world, the circumstances you face, and your intellectual capabilities. Communication—your ability to organize and express your thoughts.	Functioning well/ not functioning well	taking actions that express your true feelings and finding ways to be compassionate, nurturing, and care-giving to yourself and to others.

EXPRESSION

Themes based on how you express yourself or learn self-expression

Theme	Motivation	Life issues, aspects, fields of activity	Blessing/challenge	Honor the dream by
4: How do you express your feelings and compassion and develop a sense of "home"?	Issues dealing with sensitivity, caring, love, or applied wisdom	Feeling—how you express your feelings and how feelings affect you. Nurturing—how you "mother"—watch over and nourish others and yourself. Home base—a place or mental state that provides stability for you.	Being nurtured/needing care	taking actions that truly express your will, enabling you to develop creativity and passion for new discoveries.
5: How do you exert your will so that you may express creativity, explore, and discover?	Issues dealing with will, determination, or use of power	Creativity—how you express your innate personal creativity, and how you remove limitations that inhibit your creativity. Will—deciding what you want and choosing courses of action to get you there. Romance—learning about what you love and seeking ways to express that love, while still holding on to your independence and will.	Unlimited opportunity/limited opportunity	taking actions that improve personal analytical skills, looking for ways to improve the service work you do on the job, or seeking new challenges.
6: How do you use your analytical skills to develop confidence and meet challenges?	Issues dealing with thought, reason, or adaptability	Self-confidence—assurance within yourself that you have potential and all the analytical skills you need to adapt and meet the challenges of life. Challenges—the tests that life gives you; crises and conflicts that build self-confidence and prepare you to interact with and help others. Service—applying your skills and abilities in meaningful work.	Success/failure	taking actions that involve uniting in a relationship or partnership and balancing with a person, cause, place, or work endeavor.

INTERACTION

Themes based on how you interact with others

Theme	Motivation	Life issues, aspects, fields of activity	Blessing/challenge	Honor the dream by
7: How do you achieve balance and learn to love through a partner?	Issues dealing with sensitivity, caring, love, or applied wisdom	Partnership—making a commitment to a person, cause, field of work, or belief. Love—having intense affection for and wanting to be committed to someone or something you desire. Balance—seeking harmony with something or someone you love and with whom you are in partnership. It involves give and take.	Feeling loved/feeling threatened	taking actions that involve sharing resources and desires, sharing personal will and power, or expressing yourself through others.
8: How do you let go of ego by sharing resources, yet still fulfill personal desires?	Issues dealing with will, determination, or use of power	Regeneration—death of the ego self and birth of the "true" self; finding your true identity, not influenced by family or upbringing. Joint resources—physical and interpersonal resources you share in your partnerships. Desire—your wishes and dreams; what you imagine your ideal world to be.	Revived, healed/victimized	taking actions that involve thinking from the other person's perspective and considering the future of the relationship rather than the momentary feelings or reactions.
9: How do you adapt or broaden your perspective through conceptualized thought?	Issues dealing with thought, reason, or adaptability	High consciousness—cognizance of the greater good for yourself and others; accepting responsibility for leading an ordered life. Perspective—openness and willingness to adapt to other viewpoints. Future orientation—planning and being open to potentialities and opportunities.	Mobility/immobility	taking actions that involve using what you have accomplished in your life to help others heal, transform, and experience renewal.

CAPITALIZATION

Themes based on how you capitalize on your experience

Theme	Motivation	Life issues, aspects, fields of activity	Blessing/challenge	Honor the dream by
10: How do you apply what you have learned from the past to benefit yourself and society?	Issues dealing with sensitivity, caring, love, or applied wisdom	Achievement—recognition by yourself and others of what you have accomplished and learned from your past. Using—applying what you have learned to benefit yourself and society. Transformation—converting mental, emotional, and spiritual energy into physical form; changing the nature of your world by applying your wisdom in thought, word, and deed.	Gaining from experience or improving/failing to gain from experience or falling behind	taking actions that involve humanitarianism, community-mindedness, nonattachment, and commitment to universal truths.
11: What do you know to be truly essential and of value for yourself and society?	Issues dealing with will, determination, or use of power	Community—collectivity; group identity; seeing your relationship with all of humanity. Truth—knowing what is essential and of value for yourself and humanity beyond what others say or what you read. Nonattachment—giving up attachments to petty illusions and desires.	Being guided and hopeful/being misled and fearful	taking actions that enable you to realize the freedom your beliefs give you to make choices that enable you to seek wholeness, true joy, and spontaneity.
12: What do you believe about freeing yourself from boundaries and achieving wholeness?	Issues dealing with thought, reason, or adaptability	Duality—polarization; the struggle between two opposing tendencies or possibilities. Freedom—release from voluntary or involuntary confinements or restrictions. Wholeness—integration of the different aspects of yourself; also, recognition of yourself as one with all life.	Unrestricted and in control/ restricted or overwhelmed	taking actions that involve differentiating your self-image, self-identity, and your outlook on life with renewed optimism and trust—all attributes of theme #1.

Ninety-nine Examples of Twelve

Humanity has always recognized the particular significance of the number twelve throughout history. We find twelve in all walks of life, from religion and politics to measurement and mathematics.

Numerologists and esotericists speculate on the vibrations and characteristics of the number itself. For instance, some see four plus eight to mean the world and man renewed. Twelve as four times three may represent the world and man in intimate union with God. Twelve equals three times four, suggesting the spiritual and temporal order, the esoteric and exoteric. Twelve times twelve is seen by some as the perfected soul—the Archetypal Man. Twelve is also found in many of our Platonic volumes.

Following are ninety-nine examples of twelve. You undoubtedly can find many more.

- Twelve acupuncture meridians in the body

- Twelve apostles (or disciples) in Christianity

- Twelve arts and sciences considered essential to spiritual growth by the Rosicrucians: Alchymia (alchemy), Gramatica (grammar),

Dialectica (logic), Rhetorica (oratory), Musica (music), Physica (physics), Astronomia (astronomy), Arithmetica (mathematics), Geometria (geometry), Medicina (medicine), Iurisprudentia (jurisprudence), and Theologia (theology)[19]

- Twelve as a symbol of human destiny, the product of opposing forces four (female) and three (male) for Dogons and Bambaras of Mali[20]

- Twelve branches and associated symbolic animals in the twelve yearly cycles of the Chinese calendar: the Rat, the Ox, the Tiger, the Hare, the Dragon, the Snake, the Horse, the Goat, the Monkey, the Cock, the Dog, and the Boar[21]

- The twelve chakra system predicted in New Age literature

- Twelve Celestial Hierarchies

- Twelve corners of the icosahedron

- Twelve days of duel between Chaos and Cosmos in the Sumero-Semitic tradition

- Twelve days of chaos of Saturnalia in the Graeco-Roman tradition; the dead return during the twelve nights; "these celebrations are also found in Vedic, Chinese, Pagan and European symbolism"[22]

- Twelve days of Yuletide and Christmas

- Twelve deities on Ra's solar boat (Egyptian)[23]

- Twelve descendants of Ali, the Imams, or "directors," who rule the twelve hours of the day (Islamic)[24]

- Twelve disciples of Mithra[25]

- Twelve edges of the cube, or hexahedron

- Twelve edges of the octahedron

- Twelve elders or Presbyters in the Presbyterian Church; the circle of twelve elders, the presbytery of elected leaders, was the foundation of the Protestant reformation

- Twelve entrances or portals to be passed through in the Great Pyramid before reaching the highest degree

- Twelve episodes of Moses's life

- Twelve exploits of Odysseus

- Twelve *flamines minores* followed the Pontifex Maximus at sacred rites[26]

- Twelvefold Deity, the Divine Duodecimo, manifested in the tangible created Universe as prophets, patriarchs, tribes, and apostles (Jewish and Christian writings)[27]

- Twelvefold symmetry in the snowflake

- Twelve followers of Odin

- Twelve fruits of the Cosmic Tree, the Tree of Life

- Twelve Fruits of the Spirit (Christian)

- Twelve-gated Temple planned by the Essenes of the Qumran monastery, one for each of the tribes[28]

- Twelve gates and foundation stones of the Holy City, the Heavenly Jerusalem (Revelation 21:12, 14)

- Twelve gates of hell, in which Ra spends the hours of the night (Egyptian)[29]

- Twelve gates of the Ming-t'ang[30]

- Twelve gods and goddesses of Olympus, according to Herodotus (Graeco-Roman)[31]

- Twelve gods divided the world in Plato's *Crilias*[32]

- Twelve heavenly bodies in our solar system claimed by the Sumerians: the Sun, Earth, Moon, Mercury, Venus, Mars, Jupiter, Saturn, Uranus, Neptune, Pluto, and a twelfth, Marduk[33]

- Twelve holy animals, now known as constellations[34]

- Twelve hours of the day and night, adopted independently by China, Babylon, Egypt, Greece, and India (the Greeks called them "Babylonian hours")[35]

- Twelve inches to a foot, symbolically the foot of the divine king

- Twelve Knights of King Arthur's Round Table

- Twelve Labors (exploits) of Gilgamesh

- Twelve Labors of Hercules

- Twelve lines radiating from the center of a cuboctahedron like a truss

- Twelve loaves of shew bread placed on the table in the inner court of the Tabernacle, representing the months of the year (Leviticus 24:5–9)

- Twelve mandarins governing the twelve regions of China, third millennium BC[36]

- Twelve members, or Namshans, on the Round Council of the Dalai Lama[37]

- Twelve meridians on the globe

- Twelve-mile limit, the offshore boundary of a state

- Twelve minor prophets: Amos, Haggai, Obadiah, Zechariah, Nahum, Joel, Habakkuk, Malachi, Hosea, Zephaniah, Micah, and Jonah

- Twelvemo or duodecimo, a book size of about 5 by 7¾ inches, determined by printing on sheets folded to form twelve leaves and twenty-four pages

- Twelve months of the year

- Twelve months of the year and torments in the Hermetic tradition[38]

- Twelve nations of the Commonwealth of Independent States (the former U.S.S.R.)

- Twelve nidanas, or states of emergence, symbolic of the twelve divisions or departments of the Cycle of Life in the Buddhist tradition[39]

- Twelve Norse gods

- Twelve-note chromatic scale of civilized music

- Twelve o'clock high (aircraft direction), dramatized in the 1949 WWII film starring Gregory Peck

- Twelve original and perfect points in Masonry

- Twelve oxen bearing brazen sea at Temple of Solomon (Old Testament)

- Twelve paladins or peers of Charlemagne (Celtic)[40]

- Twelve pair of cranial nerves

- Twelve patriarchs

- Twelve pence to the shilling and twelve shillings to the pound sterling (British monetary system from the Court of Charlemagne to adoption of the metric system in 1971)[41]

- Twelvepenny nail, a nail of 3¼ inches, from the original price per one hundred

- Twelve pentagonal faces to a dodecahedron

- Twelve-person jury

- Twelve points of heaven mentioned in Revelation

- Twelve points or sides to a dodecagon

- Twelve princes of the children of Israel (Old Testament)

- Twelve representing the entire Church in the Christian tradition[42]

- Twelve rivers flowing from the spring Hvergelmir (Norse)[43]

- Twelve running springs in Helim (Old Testament)[44]

- Twelve sacred Chinese ornaments[45]

- Twelve saviors (*Pistis Sophia*)[46]

- Twelve Sephira on the Tree of Life (Kabalah)

- Twelve sibyls, or classical prophetesses, adopted by mediaeval monks, each with a separate prophecy and distinct emblem[47]

- Twelve single letters in the Hebrew alphabet

- Twelve sons of Jacob who gave their name to the twelve tribes of Israel (Old Testament)

- Twelve spaces between knots on Druid's Knot[48]

- Twelve spies sent out by Moses (Old Testament)

- Twelve stars crown the Virgin of the Immaculate Conception and the Queen of Heaven (Revelation 12:1)

- Twelve stars in the bride's crown (Revelation 12:1)

- Twelve stations of Christ's Passion (New Testament)

- Twelve steps of Alcoholics Anonymous and similar programs

- Twelve stones in the outer ring of the Native American medicine wheel

- Twelve stones in the prayer circles of Gilgol erected by Moses during the desert wanderings of the Jews to maintain a covenant with divinity

- Twelve stones or jewels of the breastplate worn by the High Priest, Aaron (Old Testament)

- Twelve stones on Hebrew altar (Old Testament)

- Twelve stones taken out of the Jordan (Old Testament)

- Twelve swans swimming in the fountain of Urdar, representing the twelve original states of existence (Norse)[49]

- Twelve tables of the law (Graeco-Roman)[50]

- Twelfth Day, the twelfth day after Christmas, January 6, on which the festival of Epiphany is celebrated, formerly observed as the last day of the Christmas festivities

- Twelfth Night, the evening before Twelfth Day, formerly observed with various festivities

- Twelfthtide, the season of Twelfth Night and Twelfth Day

- Twelve-tiered Atlantean Temple of Oralin, geomancy headquarters[51]

- Twelve tissue salts[52]

- Twelve Titans, according to Hesiod (Graeco-Roman)[53]

- Twelve-tone music, relating to the traditional twelve chromatic tones; twelve-tone music relates to compositions which evolved in the 1920s based on a particular ordering (called a series or row) of the twelve pitches that constitute the diatonic scale divided into equal semitones—a type of serial music

- Twelve total of sides on two dice

- Twelve towns surrounding the Sea of Galilee, all prominent in the life and activity of Christ

- Twelve tribes of Israel

- Twelve zodiacal signs or aspects, seen as adityas or aeons in Indian astrology, branches of the fruit tree in Arabian astrology, deities in Hindu astrology, and Olympian gods and goddesses in Greek astrology

Endnotes

1. Moore, Thomas, *Care of the Soul* (New York: HarperCollins Publishers, Inc., 1992), 13.

2. Michell, John, *Twelve-Tribe Nations and the Science of Enchanting the Landscape* (Grand Rapids, MI: Phanes Press, 1991).

3. Kushi, Michio, *Nine Star Ki* (Becket, MA: One Peaceful World Press, 1991), 22 (numbers added for clarity).

4. Rudhyar, Dane, *An Astrological Mandala: The Cycle of Transformation and Its 360 Symbolic Phases* (New York: Vintage Books, 1974), 30–31.

5. Spiritual scholars may recognize these three types of energy as being similar to the first three of what are known as the Seven Rays. Ray 1 is will and power, ray 2 is love and wisdom, and ray 3 is intelligent activity. These three are said to constitute all of divine manifestation. Many books are available describing the rays. The most authentic and informative of these books are published by the Lucis Publishing Company, 120 Wall Street, New York, NY 10005.

6. Taylor, Jeremy, *Where People Fly and Water Runs Uphill* (New York: Warner Books, Inc., 1992), 11.

7. Myss, Caroline, *Spiritual Madness: The Necessity of Meeting God in Darkness* (cassettes) (Boulder: Sounds True, 1997), tape 1, side A.

8. Ullman, Montague, MD, and Nan Zimmerman, *Working with Dreams* (Los Angeles: Jeremy P. Tarcher, Inc., 1979), 206.

9. Adler, Vera Stanley, *The Finding of the Third Eye* (New York: Samuel Weiser, 1973), 146–147.

10. Parrish-Harra, Carol E., *Adventure in Meditation: Spirituality for the 21st Century, Volume I* (Tahlequah, OK: Sparrow Hawk Press, 1995), 70.

11. Tonay, Veronica, *The Art of Dreaming* (Berkeley: Celestial Arts Publishing, 1995), 60. (The new title for this book is *The Creative Dreamer: Using Your Dreams to Unlock Your Creativity.*)

12. Tonay, 64–65.

13. Bosnak, Robert, *Tracks in the Wilderness of Dreaming* (New York: Delacorte Press, 1996), 163–205.

14. Bosnak, 166.

15. Born, Margot, *Seven Ways to Look at a Dream* (Washington, DC: Starrhill Press, 1991).

16. Savary, Louis M., Patricia H. Berne, and Strephon Kaplan Williams, *Dreams and Spiritual Growth* (Mahwah, NJ: Paulist Press, 1984).

17. Taylor, Jeremy, *Where People Fly and Water Runs Uphill* (New York: Warner Books, Inc., 1992), 11.

18. The actual quote by Rumi, translated by Coleman Barks, is as follows:

I am so small I can barely be seen.
How can this great love be inside me?
Look at your eyes. They are small,
but they see enormous things.

19. Hall, Manly P., *The Secret Teachings of All Ages* (Los Angeles: The Philosophical Research Society, Inc., 1988), CXLIV.

20. Chevalier, Jean, and Alain Gheerbrant, *The Penguin Dictionary of Symbols* (London: Penguin Books, Ltd., 1996), 1044.

21. Cooper, J. C., *An Illustrated Encyclopaedia of Traditional Symbols* (New York: Thames and Hudson, Ltd., 1995), 200.

22. Cooper, 120.

23. Howell, Alice O., *Jungian Symbolism in Astrology* (London: The Theosophical Publishing House, 1987), 79.

24. Cooper, 120.

25. Ibid.

26. Ibid.

27. Hall, CXXXVI.

28. Michell, John, and Christine Rhone, *Twelve-Tribe Nations and the Science of Enchanting the Landscape* (Grand Rapids: Phanes Press, 1991), 79.

29. Cooper, 120.

30. Howell, 79.

31. Cooper, 120.

32. Michell, 81.

33. Sitchin, Zecharia, *The 12th Planet* (New York: Avon Books, 1976), 234–235.

34. Hall, LXXXVIII.

35. Schneider, Michael S., *A Beginner's Guide to Constructing the Universe: The Mathematical Archetypes of Nature, Art, and Science* (New York: HarperCollins Publishers, Inc., 1995), 209.

36. Michell, 12.

37. Schneider, 204.

38. Cooper, 120.

39. Gaskell, G. A., *Dictionary of All Scriptures and Myths* (Avenel, NJ: Gramercy Books, 1981), 534.

40. Cooper, 120.

41. Schneider, 209.

42. Ferguson, George, *Signs & Symbols in Christian Art* (New York: Oxford University Press, 1961), 154.

43. Howell, 79.

44. Ibid.

45. Ibid.

46. Ibid.

47. Cooper, J. C, ed., *Brewer's Myth and Legend* (London: Cassell Publishers Limited, 1992), 264.

48. Howell, 79.

49. Gaskell, 780.

50. Cooper, J. C., *An Illustrated Encyclopaedia of Traditional Symbols* (New York: Thames and Hudson, Ltd., 1995), 120.

51. Leviton, Richard, "Ley Lines & the Meaning of Adam," paper in *Anti-Gravity & the World Grid* (Kempton, IL: Adventures Unlimited Press, 1995), 192.

52. Howell, 79.

53. Cooper, 120.

Suggested Readings

Abraham, Kurt. *Threefold Method for Understanding the Seven Rays.* Cape May, NJ: Lampus Press, 1984.

Ackroyd, Eric. *A Dictionary of Dream Symbols; with an Introduction to Dream Psychology.* London: Blandford, 1993.

Adler, Vera Stanley. *The Finding of the Third Eye.* New York: Samuel Weiser, 1973.

Bailey, Alice A., and Tibetan Master Djwhal Khul, compiled by a student. *The Seven Rays of Life.* London: Lucis Publishing Company, 1995.

Bolen, Jean Shinoda. *Goddesses in Everywoman.* New York: Harper-Perennial, 1984.

———. *Gods in Everyman.* San Francisco: Harper & Row, 1989.

Born, Margot. *Seven Ways to Look at a Dream.* Washington, DC: Starrhill Press, 1991.

Bosnak, Robert. *Tracks in the Wilderness of Dreaming.* New York: Delacorte Press, 1996.

Bunker, Dusty. *Numerology, Astrology and Dreams.* Atglen, PA: Whitford Press, 1987.

Burt, Kathleen. *Archetypes of the Zodiac*. St. Paul: Llewellyn Publications, 1997.

Campbell, Joseph. *The Hero with a Thousand Faces*. Princeton, NJ: Princeton University Press, 1949.

Clift, Jean Dalby, and Wallace B. Clift. *Symbols of Transformation in Dreams*. New York: The Crossword Publishing Company, 1989.

———. *The Hero Journey in Dreams*. New York: Crossword Publishing Company, 1991.

Delaney, Gayle. *All About Dreams*. San Francisco: HarperSanFrancisco, 1998.

———. *In Your Dreams*. San Francisco: HarperSanFrancisco, 1997.

Faraday, Ann. *The Dream Game*. New York: Harper & Row, 1974.

Feinstein, David, and Stanley Krippner. *Personal Mythology*. Los Angeles: Jeremy P. Tarcher, Inc., 1988.

Garfield, Patricia. *The Universal Dream Key*. New York: HarperCollins Publishers, 2001.

Gaskell, G. A. *Dictionary of All Scriptures and Myths*. New York: Gramercy Books, 1981.

Gettings, Fred. *The Arkana Dictionary of Astrology*. London: Penguin Books, Ltd., 1985.

Guiley, Rosemary Ellen. *Dreamspeak: How to Understand the Messages in Your Dreams*. New York: Berkley Books, 2001.

———. *The Dreamer's Way: Using Proactive Dreaming to Heal and Transform Your Life*. New York: Berkley Books, 2004.

Guttman, Ariel, and Kenneth Johnson. *Mythic Astrology: Archetypal Powers in the Horoscope*. St. Paul: Llewellyn Publications, 1996.

Hall, James A. *Jungian Dream Interpretation.* Toronto: Inner City Books, 1983.

———. *Patterns of Dreaming: Jungian Techniques in Theory and Practice.* Boston: Shambhala Publications, Inc., 1991.

Howell, Alice O. *Jungian Symbolism in Astrology.* Wheaton, IL: The Theosophical Publishing House, 1987.

Jung, C. G. *The Undiscovered Self with Symbols and the Interpretation of Dreams.* Princeton, NJ: Princeton University Press, 1990.

Keen, Sam, and Anne Valley-Fox. *Your Mythic Journey.* Los Angeles: Jeremy P. Tarcher, Inc., 1973.

Krippner, Stanley, and Joseph Dillard. *Dreamworking: How to Use Your Dreams for Creative Problem-Solving.* Buffalo, NY: Bearly Limited, 1988.

Kripper, Stanley, Fariba Bogzaran, and André Percia de Carvalho. *Extraordinary Dreams and How to Work with Them.* Albany, NY: State University of New York Press, 2002.

Kushi, Michio. *Nine Star Ki.* Becket, MA: One Peaceful World Press, 1991.

Michell, John. *Twelve-Tribe Nations and the Science of Enchanting the Landscape.* Grand Rapids, MI: Phanes Press, 1991.

Moore, Robert, and Douglas Gillette. *King, Warrior, Magician, Lover.* San Francisco: HarperSanFrancisco, 1990.

———. *The King Within.* New York: Avon Books, 1992.

Moore, Thomas. *Care of the Soul.* New York: HarperCollins Publishers, Inc., 1992.

Moss, Robert. *Conscious Dreaming: A Spiritual Path for Everyday Life.* New York: Crown Trade Paperbacks, 1996.

Myss, Caroline. *Sacred Contracts: Awakening Your Divine Potential.* New York: Harmony Books, 2001.

———. *Spiritual Madness: The Necessity of Meeting God in Darkness* (cassettes). Boulder, CO: Sounds True, 1997.

Oken, Alan. *Alan Oken's Complete Astrology.* New York: Bantam Books, 1988.

Parrish-Harra, Carol E. *Adventure in Meditation: Spirituality for the 21st Century, Volume I.* Tahlequah, OK: Sparrow Hawk Press, 1995.

Pearson, Carol S. *Awakening the Heroes Within.* New York: Harper-Collins Publishers, 1991.

Robertson, Robin. *Jungian Archetypes.* York Beach, ME: Nicolas-Hays, Inc., 1995.

Rudhyar, Dane. *An Astrological Mandala: The Cycle of Transformation and Its 360 Symbolic Phases.* New York: Vintage Books, 1974.

———. *The Astrological Houses.* Sebastopol, CA: CRCS Publications, 1972.

Savary, Louis M., Patricia H. Berne, and Strephon Kaplan Williams. *Dreams and Spiritual Growth.* Mahwah, NJ: Paulist Press, 1984.

Stevens, Anthony. *Private Myths: Dreams and Dreaming.* Cambridge: Harvard University Press, 1995.

Taylor, Jeremy. *Dream Work: Techniques for Discovering the Creative Power in Dreams.* New York: Paulist Press, 1983.

———. *The Living Labyrinth.* New York: Paulist Press, 1998.

———. *Where People Fly and Water Runs Uphill.* New York: Warner Books, Inc., 1992.

Tonay, Veronica. *The Art of Dreaming*. Berkeley, CA: Celestial Arts Publishing, 1995. (Also under the title *The Creative Dreamer: Using Your Dreams to Unlock Your Creativity.*)

Ullman, Montague, and Nan Zimmerman. *Working with Dreams*. Los Angeles: Jeremy P. Tarcher, Inc., 1979.

Ullman, Montague, and Stanley Krippner. *Dream Telepathy*. Baltimore: Penguin Books, Inc., 1974.

Van de Castle, Robert L. *Our Dreaming Mind*. New York: Ballantine Books, 1994.

Additional Resources

Dream Network (periodical)
   1337 Powerhouse Lane, Suite 22
   PO Box 1026
   Moab, UT 84532-5936
   Website: www.DreamNetwork.net
   E-mail: publisher@dreamnetwork.net

The Haden Institute (offers two-year dream leader training and other intensives)
   Bob Haden
   PO Box 1793
   Flat Rock, NC 28731-1793
   Website: www.hadeninstitute.com
   E-mail: bob@hadeninstitute.com

The International Association for the Study of Dreams
   IASD Central Office
   4644 Geary Boulevard
   San Francisco, CA 94118
   Website: www.asdreams.org
   E-mail: office@asdreams.org

John F. Kennedy University (offers programs in dream studies)
   100 Ellinwood Way
   Pleasant Hill, CA 94523-4817
   Website: www.jfku.edu
   E-mail: holistic@jfku.edu

The New England Dreamwork Institute (dreamwork training in Massachusetts and California)
   Cody Sisson
   330 Old Wendell Road
   Northfield, MA 01360
   Website: www.dragon-heart.com
   E-mail: cody@dragon-heart.com

Pacifica Graduate Institute (programs in psychology and mythological studies)
   249 Lambert Road
   Carpinteria, CA 93013
   Website: www.pacifica.edu

Index

Power
   As motivator of dream characters, 19, 42, 56, 72, 75
   As theme aspect, 35, 43, 44, 75–76, 112–114, 117, 121–122
Precognitive dreams, 8–9
Present tense, 21–24, 27–28, 56, 60–61, 106
Purpose, as motivator of dream characters, 16, 19, 26

Q

Question(s)
   Themes stated as, 20, 23, 27, 32, 56, 72

R

Reason, as motivator of dream characters, 19–20, 42, 56, 72, 75
Recording day notes, 52–55
Recording dream(s), 58, 60–62
Recording theme(s) of the day, 55–59
Recurring dreams/themes, 4–5, 82–87, 89–90, 106–107, 109
Regeneration, 38, 45
Reminiscing on themes, 52, 86, 90, 93, 107
Resources
   Joint/shared, 38, 45, 122–124
   Personal, 35, 44, 58–59, 113–114
Responsibility, 38, 45, 49–50, 65, 80, 125–127
Romance, 37, 44

Rudhyar, Dane, 11–12
Rumi, 127

S

Sancta Sophia Seminary, 57
Savary, Louis M., 5, 98
Safety, 35, 44, 76, 113
Security, 35, 41, 44, 112–115
Self-confidence, 37, 44, 120
Self-identity, 6, 35, 44, 112, 131–132
Self-reliance, 35, 41, 44, 46, 79, 113–115
Sensitivity, as motivator of dream characters, 19, 27, 42–45, 47, 56, 72, 75
Service(s)
   As theme aspect, 37, 44, 57–58, 118–119, 122–123
   In daily review, 57
Shared resources, 38, 45, 122–124
Soul purpose, 7
Spontaneity, 128, 131
Sparrow Hawk Village, 57
Stabilization, 12
Storytelling, 4
Subconscious, 47, 54, 58, 60, 74, 87, 95, 100, 106–107
Success, 37, 59
Sumerians, 10
Symbol(s)/symbolism, 2–4, 6, 54, 72, 82, 84, 90, 99, 101
Synthesize/ synthesizing, 36, 41, 44, 77, 88, 115

Dreams

Working Interactive

Stephanie Jean Clement, Ph.D.
and Terry Rosen

Dreams is the only complete and interactive system for helping you determine the unique, personal meaning of your dreams. What does it mean to dream of the house you grew up in? Why do certain people appear in your dreams again and again? How can you tell if a dream is revealing the future? Together, the book and software program provide everything necessary to effectively record and analyze whatever message your subconscious throws your way.

Absent in *Dreams* is the psychological jargon that makes many dream books so difficult. Examples of dreams illustrate the various types of dreams, and each chapter gives information about how to identify and work with dream symbols. The software program gives you the capacity to print out your dreams, incorporating the symbol definitions you select. What's more, the program will facilitate further exploration of your dreams with suggestions and questions.

1-56718-145-7

240 pp., 7½ x 9⅛, CD-ROM software for Windows $24.95

Dreams and What They Mean to You
MIGENE GONZÁLEZ-WIPPLER

Everyone dreams. Yet dreams are rarely taken seriously—they seem to be only a bizarre series of amusing or disturbing images that the mind creates for no particular purpose. Yet dreams, through a language of their own, contain essential information about ourselves which, if properly analyzed and understood, can change our lives. In this fascinating and well-written book, the author gives you all of the information needed to begin interpreting—even creating—your own dreams.

Dreams and What They Mean To You begins by exploring the nature of the human mind and consciousness, then discusses the results of the most recent scientific research on sleep and dreams. The author analyzes different types of dreams: telepathic, nightmares, sexual, and prophetic. In addition, there is an extensive dream dictionary that lists the meanings for a wide variety of dream images.

Most importantly, González-Wippler tells you how to practice creative dreaming—consciously controlling dreams as you sleep. Once a person learns to control his dreams, his horizons will expand and his chances of success will increase!

0-87542-288-8
240 pp., mass market $4.99

Spanish edition:
Sueños: Lo que significan para usted
1-56718-881-8 $7.95

To order, call 1-877-NEW-WRLD
Prices subject to change without notice

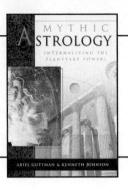

Mythic Astrology
Internalizing the Planetary Powers

ARIEL GUTTMAN & KENNETH JOHNSON

Enter a new dimension of spiritual self-discovery when you probe the mythic archetypes represented in your astrological birth chart. Myth has always been closely linked with astrology. Experience these myths and gain a deeper perspective on your eternal self.

Learn how the characteristics of the gods developed into the meanings associated with particular planets and signs. Look deeply into your own personal myths, and enjoy a living connection to the world of the deities within you. When you finally stand in the presence of an important archetype (through the techniques of dreamwork, symbolic amplification, or active imagination described in the book), you will have the opportunity to receive a message from the god or goddess.

0-87542-248-9
400 pp., 7 x 10, illus. $24.95

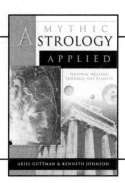

Mythic Astrology Applied
Personal Healing Through the Planets

ARIEL GUTTMAN & KENNETH JOHNSON

The gods and goddesses of the ancient world are still with us today. They act out in our celebrities, the media, and most of all within our ourselves—often through our dreams and our own horoscopes. Through the planets in your chart you can discover the mythic dimensions of your own life. The authors of Mythic Astrology provide a way to do just that in their new book, *Mythic Astrology Applied*. Learn how to contact, work with, and bring harmony to the planetary archetypes within yourself.

This book might have you saying things like: "Now I know why I married a Vesta but really long for a Venus as my partner," or "Now I understand my relationship with my mother; she is a Demeter and I'm a Persephone."

0-7387-0425-3
360 pp., 7 x 10, illus. $24.95

Tarot & Dream Interpretation

JULIE GILLENTINE
FOREWORD BY MARY K. GREER

The Tarot is both a symbolic alphabet and a book of wisdom that speaks directly to the subconscious. Dreams speak to us in the same way, namely in symbols of a universal nature.

By integrating these two ancient and potent methods of symbolic communication, you can enhance your ability to decode the nightly messages from your soul and use your dream time as a source of spiritual enlightenment.

Learn how to keep a dream journal, meditate in preparation for dream work, and select from the author's Tarot spreads for decoding different types of dreams. Explore the meanings of the Major and Minor Arcana as they pertain to dreams, and use the Symbol Dictionary as a guide to common dream themes.

0-7387-0220-X
240 pp., 6 x 9, illus. $14.95

All Around the Zodiac

Exploring Astrology's Twelve Signs

Bil Tierney

A fresh, in-depth perspective on the zodiac you thought you knew. This book provides a revealing new look at the astrological signs, from Aries to Pisces. Gain a deeper understanding of how each sign motivates you to grow and evolve in consciousness. How does Aries work with Pisces? What does Gemini share in common with Scorpio? *All Around the Zodiac* is the only book on the market to explore these sign combinations to such a degree.

Not your typical Sun sign guide, this book is broken into three parts. Part 1 defines the signs, part 2 analyzes the expression of sixty-six pairs of signs, and part 3 designates the expression of the planets and houses in the signs.

0-7387-0111-4
528 pp., 6 x 9 $17.95

The Sabian Symbols
& Astrological Analysis
The Original Symbols Fully Revealed

BLAIN BOVEE

The Sabian symbols are a set of 360 channeled images corresponding to the degrees of the zodiac. A rich source of wisdom and inspiration, these symbols are indispensable for astrological analysis. *The Sabian Symbols & Astrological Analysis* offers an insightful look at the Sabian symbols, based on the original notations of their creator, Marc Edmund Jones.

Discussing each degree of the zodiac, Blain Bovee helps readers understand the Sabian symbols, while leaving plenty of room for individual interpretation. The extensive use of key words and phrases prompts the reader to use a creative approach and to find the relevance of a specific symbol to his or her life. Bovee also demonstrates how to draw meaning from astrological pairs and opposing degrees.

0-7387-0530-6
312 pp., 7½ x 9⅛   **$19.95**

Gypsy Dream Dictionary
RAYMOND BUCKLAND

The world of dreams is as fascinating as the world of the Gypsies themselves. The Gypsies carried their arcane wisdom and time-tested methods of dream interpretation around the world. Now Raymond Buckland, a descendant of the Romani Gypsies, reveals their fascinating methods. You will learn how to interpret the major symbols and main characters in your dreams to decipher what your subconscious is trying to tell you.

You will also discover how to direct your dreams through "lucid dreaming," the art of doing whatever you want in your dream, as you dream it! Practice astral projecting in your dreams . . . travel to new places or meet with friends at a predetermined location!

1-56718-090-6
240 pp., 5³⁄₁₆ x 6 $7.95

To Write to the Author

If you wish to contact the author or would like more information about this book, please write to the author in care of Llewellyn Worldwide and we will forward your request. Both the author and publisher appreciate hearing from you and learning of your enjoyment of this book and how it has helped you. Llewellyn Worldwide cannot guarantee that every letter written to the author can be answered, but all will be forwarded. Please write to:

Robert P. Gongloff
℅ Llewellyn Worldwide
2143 Wooddale Drive, Dept. 0-7387-0818-6
Woodbury, MN 55125-2989, U.S.A.
Please enclose a self-addressed stamped envelope for reply,
or $1.00 to cover costs. If outside U.S.A., enclose
international postal reply coupon.

Many of Llewellyn's authors have websites with additional information and resources. For more information, please visit our website at http://www.llewellyn.com.